W9-BTR-894

21 DAYS TO RESILIENCE

How to Transcend the Daily Grind,
Deal with the Tough Stuff,
and Discover Your Strongest Self

Zelana Montminy, Psy.D.

HarperOne
An Imprint of HarperCollinsPublishers

HarperOne

HarperCollins books may be purchased for educational, business, or sales promotional use. For information please e-mail the Special Markets Department at SPsales@harpercollins.com.

HarperCollins website: http://www.harpercollins.com

FIRST EDITION

Designed by Claudia Smelser

Library of Congress Cataloging-in-Publication Data

Names: Montminy, Zelana, author.

Title: 21 days to resilience : how to transcend the daily grind, deal with the tough stuff, and discover your strongest self / Zelana Montminy.

Other titles: Twenty one days to resilience

Description: n : HarperElixir, 2016. | Description based on print version record and CIP data provided by publisher; resource not viewed.

Identifiers: LCCN 2016005188 (print) | LCCN 2015049478 (ebook) | ISBN 978-0-06-242878-3 (e-book) | ISBN 978-0-06-242877-6 (hardback) | ISBN 978-0-06-247029-4 (audio)

Subjects: LCSH: Resilience (Personality trait) | Adjustment (Psychology) | BASIC: SELF-HELP / Personal Growth / Happiness. | BODY, MIND & SPIRIT / Inspiration & Personal Growth. | PSYCHOLOGY / Emotions.

Classification: LCC BF698.35.R47 (print) | LCC BF698.35.R47 M66 2016 (ebook) DDC 158.1—dc23

LC record available at http://lccn.loc.gov/2016005188

16 17 18 19 20   RRD(H)   10 9 8 7 6 5 4 3 2 1

To Joel, Ethan, and Ava—
You are my light, my hope, my heart.

Contents

Introduction

....

When one door of happiness closes, another opens;
but often we look so long at the closed door that we do not
see the one which has been opened for us.

HELEN KELLER

A few years ago, a headline in the *New York Times* caught my attention: *What If the Secret to Success Is Failure?* The article was about how two principals at very different schools—one was the head of a charter school with diverse low-income students, and the other, the head of a private school that had mostly affluent students—were working together to better their students' chances for success.

The article quoted the charter school's principal on who he thought would succeed, and it wasn't going to be the kids who got the best grades. It wasn't the happiest ones, the ones who had the strongest social skills, or those who rated highest on intelligence tests. It was "the ones who were able to recover from a bad grade and resolve to do better next time; to bounce back from a fight with their parents and work through it better next time; to resist the urge to go out to the movies and stay home and study instead; to persuade professors to give them extra help after classes."

It dawned on me that the students who will succeed are resilient. I started looking more closely at resilience and quickly realized that these students share this vital skill with the strongest, most successful and content people in the world. Happiness isn't the connecting thread—but why?

We do so much of what we *think* will make us blissful but so many of us are unhappier than ever before. The code to unlocking happiness and success isn't the quest for it after all. Groundbreaking research shows that happiness is in fact much easier to attain if we stop focusing on it so much. Although this might sound counterintuitive, happiness shouldn't be the end goal if you really want to be happy.[1] Research has actually exposed several negative side effects of happiness, particularly that too much of the wrong type of happiness, experienced at an improper time, pursued in the wrong way, can be damaging.[2] The antidote: undertake resilience instead.

Our frantic search for happiness is leading us astray primarily because we are fixated on the wrong things. We desperately try to capture good feelings for ourselves, which alienates us from others. As contagious as happiness can be if we express it, the process of attaining it that we've primarily been taught can be a very lonesome pursuit which further decreases happiness.[3] Plus we overestimate how thrilled certain achievements are going to really make us. When we don't feel those emotions we expected, we keep striving for more and more that similarly doesn't produce the feelings we hope for, continuing a vicious cycle. In this way, a focus on happiness mostly serves to highlight our shortcomings. Lasting happiness requires building upon your strengths, persevering, and being gracious with yourself and others—it's really not about personal achievements or experiencing fleeting positive thoughts and feelings.

The words "happiness" and "resilience" get thrown around often it seems. Because of this, we've tuned out. They have lost their powerful meaning. Overuse doesn't make these concepts any less important though. In fact, they are more important than ever before in our fast-paced world. I've noticed people these days expect others to solve their problems and often blame society for their issues. In this age of instant gratification and quick results, people seem to get uncomfortable when they have to work hard and problem solve. They reject negative feelings like the plague. But that's not going to make them any happier. In fact, it's healthy—almost necessary—to sometimes not be happy in order to find lifelong well-being.

While negative feelings clearly don't *feel* good, they are important tools for growth and learning. And while our environment definitely affects our lives, it is entirely up to us to have the strength to overcome whatever is thrown at us. That vital muscle, our ability to overcome and learn from our challenges—resilience—is often neglected. We need to become more resilient to ultimately be happy. I wrote this book to help you do that.

We're still learning more about the complex trait of resilience every day. Recent research has begun to identify its environmental, neurological, and even possible genetic sources. Although there is much that we still don't know about it, we do know that it's not *entirely* genetic. While some people have an easier time turning trauma into triumphs, resilience is a skill we can all develop. It is not a fixed state of being.[4] We can build it and continue to work on it just like we can train our brain to be more positive and optimistic. In fact, positive emotions play a large role in resilience. Research has shown that they help us rebound better from trauma and find opportunities for growth from stressful experiences.[5]

Being resilient does not mean that you won't encounter problems or have difficulties overcoming a challenge in your life. The difference is that resilient people don't let their adversity *define* them. At its core, resilience is about being capable and strong enough to persevere in adverse or stressful conditions—and to take away positive meaning from that experience.

Living with resilience is more than just "bouncing back"; it is about shifting our perceptions, changing our responses, and experiencing real growth. Louis Zamperini, whom I had the pleasure of meeting and having dinner with, is one of the greatest examples of this. His story of endurance and survival was well documented in the bestselling book and movie *Unbroken*. An Olympic runner, Louie fought in World War II, during which he survived a horrific plane crash and seven weeks at sea adrift in the Pacific on a flimsy raft, only to be taken prisoner and forced to endure horrendous conditions in Japanese

POW camps. Through it all, he maintained his courage and hope. When I met him a few years ago before he died, he had this twinkle in his eye, and his ever-present zest for life was palpable—Louis is the epitome of resilience. He taught me that through our human frailties and due to factors entirely out of our control, we must accept and deal in real time with our flawed existence and our circumstances as they are, not as what we want them to be. The only thing we have control over is that we have the ability to definitively and consciously change how we respond to what life throws at us at any given moment. We all endure challenges, big and small, which are meaningful opportunities for learning and building strength.

One of the most remarkable studies on resilience was published in 2003. In late August 2001, researchers recruited college students for a study measuring resilience and other psychological traits. But then 9/11 unexpectedly and tragically happened, and so, nine days after the attacks, researchers reconnected with participants for a follow-up study on reactions to the attacks. Because the participants' level of resilience was measured before and after the attacks, researchers had a unique opportunity to study how they coped. Participants who had scored high on resilience prior to the attacks reported greater positive emotions such as gratitude, interest, and love, even while simultaneously feeling negative emotions such as fear, anger, and sadness. Researchers also found that these highly resilient people actually increased their levels of optimism, well-being, and feelings of tranquillity and peace after 9/11.[6] This study illustrates how highly resilient people seem to not only bounce back from hard times, but also grow and become stronger as a result—they experience posttraumatic growth. They found a way for their struggle to redefine their life and fill it with new meaning. This type of growth is the cornerstone of resilience.

My Story

The quest to strengthen resilience resonates with anyone. We all face challenges—they are an important part of our journey. My life, too, is rife with them.

My parents and older sister emigrated from the Soviet Union to the United States in 1976. Many times they were told they would not be able to make it. They were diverted to Italy first. Then Chicago. They finally settled in San Diego, where I was born. Like many immigrants, they came with nothing. No money, no language. But they didn't take no for an answer. How did they make dreams their reality? Hard work, dedication, perseverance, resilience. I was raised with that mind-set and taught that anything was possible.

As the first person in my family to be born in this country, the difficult part of assuming that role was finding a balance between two very different cultures. In fourth grade, I remember wishing my family were American. How I wanted to blend in. I had not been in the world long enough to realize how my differences could be beneficial. Yet with each year that passed I realized that those very differences I feared revealing are, in fact, an integral part of me—they give me texture and dimension.

As a child, I often played with my *matryoshka,* a wooden Russian doll that has other, smaller dolls stacked inside. I would remove one after another and marvel at each new doll I discovered. It dawned on me, in subsequent years, that we are all matryoshkas, containing hidden facets, parts within parts. I, too, was a matryoshka, and instead of rejecting parts of myself that differentiated me, I began to embrace them. Part of what fascinated me about psychology early on was its ability to reveal hidden facets that make us whole. Clearly, the matryoshka doll and her inner layers still resonate.

I tried to approach my middle school social experience with a similar mind-set, remembering that everyone has a story and hidden parts that make them whole. But sometimes the bullying was too much to bear. I was targeted by a girl who happened to lead the "popular" pack. Her aggression was intentional, repeated, continual. That's what made it so hard; she didn't relent. It was almost as if she felt comfort by inflicting pain. She spread rumors, taunted and teased me. She rallied a group that was fearful of her to join in at times, excluding me at events and during lunchtime. There were many days I'd eat by myself in a bathroom stall. They'd be waiting for me outside, psychologically and verbally harassing me as I exited. Those were the toughest days.

It got progressively worse and physical, stealing my sports clothes and throwing them in the trash. Tripping me intentionally during a soccer game. I still remember a cold winter day when they stole the one jacket I had and soaked it with water in the sink, returning it to me dripping wet. It infuriated her that I wasn't openly fazed by the verbal abuse, that I often ignored her slander. When I spoke out to defend myself, she would retreat, only to unleash more horrid assaults later. It was humiliating. Heartbreaking. Debilitating at times. Still, I made some friends and there were good-hearted people who attempted to stand up for me, only to become other targets of her abuse. There were many days I didn't want to go to school even though I loved learning and my teachers; other days I just cried and cried. I blamed myself even though deep inside a part of me knew I didn't cause it.

This went on for more than a year. Pure torture. I tried everything, to ignore, defend, talking to teachers, the headmaster. We tried to come up with a plan, but the minute the girl found out I had discussed it with anyone, she knew she was winning. She was getting to me. And she kept on trying to inflict pain without relent. Her parents were financial donors to the school, and while the administration tried a bit to help, they ultimately turned a blind eye. My parents even tried calling her parents to discuss the situation and were met with similar disdain, veiled threats, and dismissal. I ultimately had to switch schools.

Earlier this year at a conference, I ran into a classmate from that period in my life whom I hadn't seen in more than twenty years. He was one of her sidekicks back in the day. Before I was even able to say hello, he looked into my eyes as tears welled up in his and told me that all these years he's thought about what she did to me, what they did, and wanted to express his most sincere apologies but didn't know how to reach me. He voiced how wrong it was, how horrific he felt. And that he was so sorry. So profoundly sorry. Needless to say, it was incredibly powerful.

Part of what I learned from that awful experience was to let the heartache be my teacher. I learned getting defeated by pain was not an option. I had to press on. My problems didn't define me. I could rise above and figure out ways to cope. I knew that only I had control of my outcome, my reactions. Maintaining a positive perspective was the way to pull through; it was my medicine. I learned to rely on self-respect, purpose, acceptance, every tool I discuss in the following chapters to survive. I knew that anything could be overcome if I tried hard enough. If I believed I could. And ultimately, I did.

I now know that my classmate was battling her own demons that caused her to lash out. She was modeling what she had been exposed to from a very young age. None of us is born a bully. We learn it. It's not me, and it never was. The one most hurt by her bullying was, in the end, herself. As acutely painful as it was at the time, this pain gave me an opportunity to build resilience in ways I didn't even know I could. And for that I'm thankful.

Preparing for Your New Competence

We all have aspects of resilience within us. This book will help you unearth it and build upon the skills and strengths you already possess. This self-actualization isn't easy, but it will change you for the better. To give yourself an advantage before you even begin the 21 days, try to clear your mind of any preconceived notions about this process. I know it's hard to do that. You will be that much more successful with this starting from a place of willingness and curiosity.

How This Book Works

There are many books out there explaining why resilience is important. This book is about *how* to build it. I'm giving you a tool kit—your very own practical day-by-day guide—that offers ways to strengthen the 21 factors that increase resilience, from social support to emotional intelligence to gratitude. It's not always going to be easy, but it is going to be transformative.

I've read and even written my fair share of academic articles, literature reviews, and even a lengthy scientific doctoral dissertation. This book is not that. Instead, I've taken all of my research, experience, and background on this topic and condensed it for you. It is all streamlined for a reason—simplicity works. It makes concepts much easier to process and build upon. It's less overwhelming for the brain to synthesize, allowing you to get ahead in a more effortless way.

This book is full of big concepts that you've probably heard about before which I've tried to explain clearly and succinctly. Many brilliant people have written about these abilities in the past. My focus is different. I'm here to help you practice and strengthen fundamental skills as a way to reinforce resilience.

This is your training manual. Don't expect to master it all right away; that's purposeful. We build physical strength gradually, and this book works the same way.

Each of the 21 traits has its own chapter. After I explain the trait and how it helps build resilience, a "Take Stock" section helps you gauge your current level of skill, and the "Daily Dos" provide tools to improve it throughout the day. Each chapter ends with a "Lifelong" exercise that offers ways to build the skill long-term.

Why 21 days? The time frame is based on a premise that it takes at least 21 days to begin the formation of a new habit.[7] But it takes at the very least two months for a new behavior to become second nature.[8] You have to do the work, and practice often, to really reap the benefits, to make resilience a way of life. This book is the first step to energizing you for lifelong change. Think of this as a three-week boot camp to hasten the resilience building process.

Each week will focus on a theme, starting with skills related to the self, moving into the next week focusing on the spirit, and closing with a week focused on social aspects. I chose to focus on the self first because it's impossible to work on other abilities without strengthening your core. Your inner being is the nucleus from which all else stems. From that, we will move on to what infuses our self with meaning and vitality—the spirit. It is our essence. Finally, in the third week we will branch out to social skills that connect, support, and ground us.

As with any learning, repetition is key. Strengthening a new muscle takes consistency, just like in the gym. You can't work out once and expect results. In the same vein, once you achieve the results you want, you can't just stop working out and expect to maintain the same muscle tone. These are simple tools that will help you build resilience and be happier. If you stick with it, and integrate them into your life consistently, you will enjoy countless benefits all around.

Let's get to it.

Week 1

SELF

Habit

···

We are what we repeatedly do. Excellence,
then, is not an act, but a habit.

ARISTOTLE

When I was pregnant with my first child, everyone used to give me unsolicited advice. It was as if my pregnant belly were a sign saying, "Please, tell me what to do! I have no clue!" Of course, family and friends offered their advice, but it wasn't just them. The cashier at the grocery store, the gardener, the aesthetician, the hairstylist—even the jogger who stopped in midrun—all had advice. I found it pretty endearing actually, sometimes even amusing. And occasionally there were some pretty helpful tips. One common suggestion was to stick to a routine, especially before bed. At the time I wondered, *What's with the dire need for all this routine?!*

Well, now a busy mom of two, I clearly see how much routine can make someone feel in control. And happy. Secure. Resilient. Without routine or if there's any change in routine, my kids are thrown off. Their behavior suffers; their sleep suffers (and so do their parents!). As a scientist, I was always curious about why children are so thrown off by a change in routine. Routines and habits signal the brain that everything is as it always is and should be; their safety net is ripped from under them as the brain notices "change." While toddlers have an extreme need for routine, it's a universal example that extends to adults as well.

We are biologically wired to need habits. Approximately 40 percent of our day is spent performing habitual, automatic tasks.[1] We're mostly on autopilot because it's easy—and reliability makes us feel safe. A new skill becomes a habit when the repetitive behavior converts into something that is mechanical, something we don't have to waste energy to even think about.[2] Good habits are healthy, protective, and productive. They help us be more resilient by providing consistency and security, so we can focus our energy on other things, such as problem solving and bouncing back from adversity. So why do people have bad habits if they're clearly not helping us in any way? Bad habits still give us a sense of comfort that makes them hard to break since they're so dependable. They are there for a reason, usually fulfilling some subconscious need. And we tend to get used to things quickly, even if they're not good for us, because we get a reward from the behavior. Behaviors such as eating even after we're full (because we're bored), watching too much

TV at night (because we're lonely or procrastinating), biting our nails (because of anxiety), looking at our phone during dinner (because we don't want to talk to anyone), and so on. We do it because that's what we've come to rely on, even when we know it's not good for us. We get addicted to the "false" reward those bad habits give us.

Resilient people know what their bad habits are and know how to break them. They replace them with better habits. They have enough control and self-awareness to do this. Fundamentally, resilient people always have a secure foundation—formed from their generally positive repetitive behaviors—to bounce back onto. They are more likely to take the initiative to fight through a challenging situation because they don't have to spend so much energy sorting through their life day to day.[3] Their positive habits support their daily functioning and free energy to focus on overcoming more demanding things.

David Karp, the founder of Tumblr, makes a list in his notebook of things that need to get done that day as he reads e-mails.[4] He's become so accustomed to this routine that he doesn't have to think about it, he just does it; it frees his brain for other, complicated tasks at hand. Every positive habit we make becomes one less positive behavior we have to think about, giving us more space and energy to engage in other positive behaviors. Oprah gives herself at least twenty minutes every day to set everything aside and meditate.[5] This daily habit allows her to feel anchored and in control, and it gives her the security to be able to deal with any adversity because she knows she can trust her daily rituals to carry her through.

Consistency is a conveyor belt that keeps us functioning. Elite athletes often rely on habits to propel their success, whether it's through habitual visualizations of crossing the finish line, consuming a particular drink before every workout, or performing a specific cool-down routine. Emily Cook, a U.S. freestyle aerial skiing Olympian, uses intense visualization throughout her training, as does much of the U.S. Olympic team and countless others.[6] Although visualizing a good outcome isn't in itself a habit, Cook has made it habitual by repeating it before every competition. Visualizing the feeling she gets when she passes the finish line, holds the gold medal in her hand, tastes the tears running down her cheeks—this habit of experiencing every detail of the future victory is an invaluable tool.

If what we do in our lives is determined much by habit, then the types of habits we have need to support the type of life we want to live. Every habit has a cue and reward that cause a certain behavior to transition from being just goal-oriented to repetitive.[7] Charles Duhigg, the author of bestseller *The Power of Habit*, explains it well, that people begin to crave the benefit of a reward when they are exposed to a certain cue or trigger. That's how a habit becomes automatic. He notes various studies that have shown people are more likely to engage in habits when done in one particular environment, but the behavior changes when out of that typical environment. This makes sense, since when we change our environment, cues change and our pattern is broken.

Knowing this framework, the cue and reward system, and learning how to break the cycle empowers us to be able to change bad habits and make good ones.[8] I used to check e-mail and news right after I woke up, before the morning rush consumed me. It was getting in the way of my productivity, and I was distracted from family time. It wasn't helpful personally or professionally. To change this habit, I took away the cue—so I now leave my phone downstairs before I go up to bed. I love the *reward* of having more time for my husband, my children, and myself in the morning. I now have no desire to check my phone immediately after waking up and sometimes even wait until after breakfast to turn it on.

Take Stock

What sort of habits do you have? Think about things you do every day. It may take more time than you think to do this, since habits can be so ingrained in our routine that you may not easily recall even doing them. What do you do right when you wake up? After that? Do you eat the same thing for breakfast every day? That's a habit, too! Take inventory of your habits, and list them below according to time of day.

- After waking _____
- Early morning _____
- Midmorning _____
- Late morning _____
- Lunchtime _____

- Early afternoon _____
- Midafternoon _____
- Late afternoon _____
- Early evening _____
- Dinnertime _____
- Before bed _____
- Bedtime _____

Once you feel the list is complete, color-code it. With a blue pen circle the good habits that you want to keep. With a red pen, circle the ones you want to change. Make a separate list of the ones you want to change, with each habit on its own line. Beside that habit, write down a habit you want to replace it with. Here's an example:

- TV before bed → book before bed
- Reaching out to spouse via text → reach out via phone
- Gym early evening after work → gym before work

Now that you have identified those habits you want to keep and what to banish from your routine, let's figure out how to keep them from sneaking back into your life.

Heads Up—Be careful not to confuse habits with goals. Habits can support goals long-term, but ultimately think of habits as a way to reach a certain goal. For example, wanting to eat healthier is a goal, not a habit. But there are many habits you can choose to support that goal, such as stocking your fridge with fresh, colorful produce, prewashed and cut so it's ready to eat, and with precooked healthy grains such as quinoa and millet so you can prepare fast and easy meals after a long day. This habit will support your goal to improve nutrition.

Daily Dos

Morning: Don't just vow to introduce a new healthy cue into your morning routine based on your current goals—also actually make it physically easier on yourself to do. If you want to start the day with a glass of warm lemon water to improve digestion and circulation, leave a lemon and cup on your kitchen counter the night before. You want to start your day with ten minutes of exercise? Leave out your yoga mat with a preset timer as a cue. If you want to start drinking tea instead of coffee, put away the coffee machine and put a tea bag in a cup by the teapot! If talking to your mom is a trigger for you to revert to childish rhetoric, wear a rubber band and snap it on your wrist when your mom calls to remind you to stay true to who you are. These are pretty straightforward—but simplicity is key here. The more complicated you make things, the harder it will be to stick with.

List three cues that trigger a new habit that you are going to introduce this week, and describe how you are going to implement them:

1. _____

2. _____

3. _____

Day: Change your environment. Think about the last time you were on vacation. I guarantee you didn't do all the same things you do at home. Perhaps you woke up and took a walk outside, instead of jumping on social media and surfing Instagram. If you'd been overeating because of anxiety or boredom at home, you didn't do that on vacation because you were with a group of people or had others at the hotel to talk with. You stopped smoking because you were too busy snorkeling. With varying surroundings, cues are different, rewards are different, and you feel different, right? Unfortunately, you can't just hop on a plane at any time, but you can take a short break from your usual routine—even just taking a walk outside will reframe your mind and help redirect habits you're looking to shift. Notice what cues change and how you want to build on that when you get back home. For example, if you didn't feel the urge to smoke while on a hike, notice what about the hike fulfilled you and made you not want to smoke. What are the cues at home or at work that make you want to smoke?

You have a pack of cigarettes by your desk or in the kitchen so visually they're apparent and available. On your hike, they weren't easily seen. You had them in your backpack and not your pocket, so you couldn't even feel them. The reward was enjoying the fresh air and not spending time doing something you know isn't good for you. Hide the cigarettes when you're back home. Replace this habit/addiction with something else that's a stress reliever, such as squeezing a soft ball in the palm of your hand. Take this time now to write down where your bad habits take place and think about an alternative location, or do more in areas where good habits take place.

_____

_____

_____

_____

_____

Evening: Quit one bad habit by taking away a cue and its reward—and have a replacement ready. For example, if you have a habit of watching TV until you fall asleep but it's impairing your sleep quality, put the remote in the bathroom before you get into bed (take away the cue). Put a good book by your bed instead (replacement). You're less likely to watch TV if it requires extra effort to get the remote and you have a good book to read next to you instead. Leave all electronics out of reach. You'll sleep better and wake up more refreshed (reward).

List five bad habits you want to change. Which cue will you take away, and what will you replace it with?

1. Habit: _____
   Cue removal: _____
   Replacement: _____

2. Habit: _____
   Cue removal: _____
   Replacement: _____

3. Habit: _____
   Cue removal: _____
   Replacement: _____

4. Habit: _____
   Cue removal: _____
   Replacement: _____

5. Habit: _____
   Cue removal: _____
   Replacement: _____

Lifelong: Changing long-held habits is not an easy feat. Often the cue that you think is triggering the habit isn't as simple as you imagine it to be.[9] A good way to filter through all the complexity is to write down details about a particular habit you're trying to change. What are you feeling at that moment? Where are you? Who's around you? What time is it? What else do you notice? Take notes every day in a separate notebook, and you'll start to see patterns. These clues will lead you to expose the cues that are spurring the habitual behavior. Once you've established this, you can plan to replace the cue with something else that will lead to a positive reward.

One of my clients wanted to change her habit of working at her desk through lunch while most of her colleagues ate together in the break room. She thought it was because she just had too much work to do. She started to write down details surrounding the habit; for example, when people would gather around noon, she would start to sweat and look down at her phone to avoid eye contact. We realized that she was actually very shy and didn't want to socialize. She still was rewarded socially by filtering through her Facebook and Instagram accounts, but it wasn't giving her the interaction she truly wanted to have. She was "hiding" at her desk, and this had become a habit. We were able to work through changing her cues, such as locating a friend to meet her in the break room before others arrived, and generated similar social rewards. This change took a lot of time and effort, but it paid off, and she now feels much more fulfilled. Habits are tough to reprogram. But understanding how habits work and knowing how to replace them with others will help you shift them for the better—and increase your resilience bit by bit.

Hope

....

Hope is important because it can make
the present moment less difficult to bear.
If we believe that tomorrow will be better,
we can bear a hardship today.

THICH NHAT HANH

I'm not a huge fan of long-distance running myself. But it's thrilling for me to watch what the human body and spirit are capable of when put to the test. The L.A. Marathon route used to pass through my neighborhood, so every year my family and I joined the cheering crowds. The runners never cease to amaze me, pushing themselves with every drop of sweat and fighting onward through the pain. I remember cheering on an amputee veteran who wheeled by. It was a ninety-degree day, sweat was pouring off his body; he was using every ounce of energy and mental toughness to push those wheels forward. Yet he smiled through the pain and his eyes glistened with joy.

The veteran was propelled by drive and heart; by hope. He and countless others there that day prompted me to think what hope and resilience are all about. What motivates us to pull through a challenge? Why should we bounce back from adversity? What's on the other side of pain? If we don't believe good will come, if we don't believe we have the ability to grow stronger, if we don't have hope in a better outcome, in a better tomorrow, then there's no reason to go on, let alone thrive. Hope is our fuel. It's our choice. Resilient people *choose* to overcome feelings of hopelessness. They don't rely on changing experiences or emotions to define their reality. They choose to look forward, to hope.

Hope is different from optimism, which is an expectation that good things will happen. Hope has to be real and profound—we can't fake it. People who lose hope lose motivation. In fact, hope has been shown to play an important role in helping people survive life-threatening diseases because hope helps people find positive meaning and the capability to imagine a future beyond their diagnosis.[1] Hope motivates survivors to fight on. I have a friend whose child was battling a powerful form of cancer. Many months and chemo treatments later, she was urged to get a screening as a precaution, and she, too, was diagnosed with cancer. It's enough to make even the strongest of us fall to the ground, never to get up again. But my friend fought hard, both for her son's survival and her own. (Both are now thriving, but not everyone is so lucky.) She and her family epitomized hope and resilience—and to fight through the darkness with such humility, grace, and courage was truly something remarkable to witness. I saw before my own eyes how believing in your very core that there is light in the future, being hopeful, can make a huge difference. Without hope, we're less likely to be resilient—to be forced to find a way out of the darkness.

Feeling hope motivates us to action. To feel hope, we need to have a positive perception of our own agency, or ability to act. We believe in ourselves enough that we'll accomplish what we set out to do. Our sense of agency is what provides the motivation to start and move toward our goal. But we also need to plan, and to trust that with that plan of action, things will ultimately turn out for the best. This combination is why hope can be tough.

We all know the dreamer in high school, who talked about moving to Los Angeles to be a movie star or to Manhattan to be a banker, but who never left home. Or those who are incredibly motivated but simply don't know how to plan. All of these people—both those who lack agency and those who lack a plan—are stuck because ultimately, they lack hope. We need to both believe that we can attain our goals (agency) and know that there are steps we can take to get there (the plan) in order to be hopeful. The two components have a reciprocal relationship—one fuels the other. Hope can also be fueled by beliefs instilled in us at an early age; telling children things like "anything is possible if you work hard enough" and reading books such as *The Little Engine That Could* have been shown to help reinforce a hopeful attitude.[2] But more often than not, beliefs related to hope are influenced by religious institutions, having strong social support, and/or cultivating an active, collaborative relationship with a greater force than oneself (charitable acts, spirituality, yoga, etc.).

Hope is good for us in a few different ways. Studies in hope theory have shown that there is a positive relationship between feeling hopeful and feeling self-worth, as well as the belief in our own capabilities. Hope also increases academic and athletic performances, physical health, and emotional intelligence—which further strengthen resilience.[3] Children who exhibit hopeful behavior have a more positive perception of their academic abilities, social acceptance, and physical appearance compared to less hopeful classmates.[4] In adults, being hopeful fuels academic success, problem solving, active coping, and most interestingly, the ability to perform athletically far beyond our natural talent. Research shows that track athletes who are hopeful tend to run faster than those who are not, and that being hopeful could be the reason why sports teams at every level succeed, despite the odds being against them.[5]

On Halloween in 2003, a young surfer named Bethany Hamilton was in the ocean off the coast of Hawaii when a tiger shark attacked her. The shark severed her left arm just below the shoulder. Only three weeks later, Bethany was back in the water relearning the sport that she loved. Just a year later, after teaching herself to surf with only her remaining arm, she entered a major surfing competition and won a national title.

In her autobiography, *Soul Surfer,* Bethany attributes her resilience to her devout religious faith—and, most tellingly, her hope for the future. Hope gave Bethany the power to bounce back from such trauma.

What gives us the kind of hope Bethany has? Our emotions grow from how we think. So if we have hopeful thoughts— even as seemingly trite as "Decide that you want it more than you are afraid of it" or "Make yesterday jealous of today"—they will help us experience more positive emotions and be more hopeful. These positive feelings and hope will fuel the motivation to create and execute the strategies needed to achieve our goals. This helps us be more resilient because positive, hopeful people face the reality of life head on and try to find solutions for current challenges. When no obvious solutions exist, they still find something else to look forward to, and to hope for. It keeps them going and helps them rebound from adversity. Researchers at the Royal Marsden Hospital in London studied women with early-stage breast cancer and found that those who didn't have hope increased their risk of recurrence or death.[6] The results were straightforward. Hopeful patients were more likely to deal with their illness themselves, and they accepted and understood all aspects of their disease. They often chose the most aggressive treatments. They were able to get through each difficult day because they had hope for a better tomorrow.

Alternatively, when we focus too much on something— constantly worrying or feeling anxious—for a long time, it prevents and paralyzes us from achieving our goals. In psychology, this behavior is called "neuroticism," and this type of negative thinking fuels more negative thinking—creating a *downward* spiral. Rumination not only prevents us from feeling hopeful, but also from having a positive perspective altogether. We can break out of this pattern by being mindful of the fact that thoughts dictate our emotions, and not the other way around.

Hope and positivity work together to fuel and build our resilience. In a 2009 study titled "Happiness Unpacked," Michael Cohn and other researchers asked a hundred volunteers to report their daily emotions online. Participants rated whether or not they experienced various emotions in the past day on a scale from 0 to 4 (not at all to extremely). Researchers asked whether participants felt amusement, awe, compassion, contentment, gratitude, hope, interest, joy, love, and/or pride, along with anger, contempt, disgust, embarrassment, fear, guilt, and sadness. Resilience was also measured. After a month, the results were compiled. Participants who had stable levels of positive emotions showed a growth in acquiring resources needed to cope, even when their days included substantial negative emotions.[7] This indicates that positive emotions and hope increase our capability to thrive despite negative circumstances—making us more resilient. Hope mobilizes us, motivates us, and keeps us moving forward.

Take Stock

Let's assess your own level of hope. Circle "yes" or "no" for the following questions.

Do you dream big?   YES NO

Do you have a realistic sense of optimism?   YES NO

Are you generally determined to reach
your goals?   YES NO

Are you creative about how you think
about problems?   YES NO

Do you find yourself planning out how to reach
your aspirations?   YES NO

Clearly, hopeful people generally answer "yes" to most of the above.

Describe below your current biggest challenge. Or what area (work, marriage, social life) you would like to work on.

_____

_____

_____

_____

_____

Assuming you are hopeful for a resolution, how have you identified ways to tackle this challenge?

_____
_____
_____
_____
_____

If you are not hopeful for a resolution, what is stopping you from being hopeful? Once you've identified your roadblocks, list three to five ways you can overcome them.

_____
_____
_____
_____
_____

Daily Dos

Morning: Hope flourishes from social connection. People who are more hopeful don't necessarily have more people around them, but they do feel more connected socially. To improve connectedness, reach out to friends and family whom you've lost touch with who are meaningful in your life. A text, note, e-mail, call, or especially a handwritten letter would go a long way in terms of reconnecting. If you're hesitant to reconnect, ask yourself why. Is it because you're hurt about something? Does this person really mean as much to you as you think? Are you unwilling to open up? What are you fearful of? What are you hiding? Don't be afraid to ask others for help, and be there to help them. It's rarely about quantity when it comes to relationships, but about quality. List three people you wish you kept in better touch with and when/how you will check in with them.

1. _____

2. _____

3. _____

Day: Using our imagination to visualize goals can help us "see" what rewards will come. "Seeing" it in our mind, even though it's not actually happening in the moment, makes us feel like it's doable and keeps us motivated and focused. Think about what *could be* rather than what is. This is very powerful. This makes our goals seem more within reach and ultimately makes it easier for us to attain them. For example, in the middle of a workday you have a conversation with your boss that makes you lose all hope of that promotion you were expecting. Turn it around and immediately visualize getting the promotion. See what that new title and office will feel like. Hear yourself telling a friend about your new role. Instead of pouting the rest of the day, this visualization will give you renewed energy, which could make you complete a task really well that gets your boss's attention for future promotions. Write down what you're going to visualize today and when. This will help get you started.

_____

_____

_____

_____

_____

_____

Night: Raise the level of hope you feel by surrounding your-self with images and messages that promote it. But don't just create a vision board of random images from magazines that appeal to you. Take the vision board exercise that you've heard about before to a deeper level by finding images or sayings that were or are currently part of your life. Find hope within what you've created for yourself, within your world. Get creative with how you display these images and sayings; it doesn't have to be on a poster board. My vision board is a collection of photos in my hallway near my bedroom that I see every day. Through various websites, you can create a collage of images to be printed on a mug or a mouse pad. Make sure your home is filled with items that you personally connect to, that are meaningful, and that remind you to have something to be hopeful for. This is a great way to give hope rebirth through connecting to significant experiences and people within our lives.

Lifelong: Nothing builds hope more than reaching goals and moving on to the next. So help yourself attain goals by making them reasonable. We audit our taxes every year. Why not our goals? Write down your top five and think about why you have them. Make sure you adjust your current goals to be realistic, achievable, and meaningful. If something seems too lofty, break it down into smaller goals that you're more likely to achieve. Are your goals in line with your purpose (see chapter 17)? Do they integrate all aspects of who you are today and who you want to be? Are they gratifying (satisfying your personal needs), or are they simply external, like making more money? Research has found that meaningful goals are easier to achieve and sustain.

Top Five Goals

1. _____

   Why? _____

2. _____

   Why? _____

3. _____

   Why? _____

4. _____

   Why? _____

5. _____

   Why? _____

Some people are prone to being more hopeful than others. If you have lost all hope, find something to believe in to help you move through the emptiness. Whether it's for another loved one, for a cause, God, for yourself. One of the hardest things to do is to trust the timing of things, especially if you're in a particularly negative place in your life. Try to move forward using my tips, and by learning and growing from each day, one moment building on to the next. Seek professional help if you're having a hard time and feel hopeless.

Health

The groundwork of all happiness is health.

LEIGH HUNT

I scratched my cornea the other day on a tree branch. The pain was brutal, and I wasn't able to see through my left eye for more than a week. Living for a week with restricted vision was definitely an eye opener (no pun intended!). We all take basic abilities for granted. We take our health for granted. Only when we get sick do most of us vow to make long-term changes. Only when we lose our abilities do we really yearn for them.

Health is everything. But it's a fundamental trait of resilience that people often forget about. When we think of the top five characteristics of resilient people, most of us would say things like they're strong, courageous, confident, optimistic, successful . . . but does "healthy" come to mind? Probably not. We've been conditioned by our culture to write off health and wellness pursuits, but I would argue it's one of the most critical aspects of resilient, happy people. They find time to exercise, they make healthy choices, and they do what they can to support their well-being because without our health, we have nothing.

So assuming we aren't sick, how does making healthy choices actually support resilience? Eating the right nutrients and staying physically active help support a strong body, a strong immune system to help fight disease, and a strong digestive system, among many other things. Resilience relies on our health to function at its best. Otherwise stress eats away at us and we break down, literally and figuratively. At its most basic level, our body is a complex machine that needs clean fuel to function at its peak. For example, having a strong digestive system and eating the right balance of nutrients help detoxification of the body, which prevents infections. We have to maintain a healthy lifestyle to be able to withstand the stress that comes with challenges.

Physical activity helps build resilience. Researchers at the National Institute for Mental Health separated male mice into two groups: aggressive and passive. The passive mice were further separated into two groups, one that exercised (with tubes, running wheels, and ladders) and a group that did not. When researchers introduced a passive mouse that didn't exercise into a cage with an aggressive mouse, the passive mouse became physiologically stressed within hours and stayed stressed after being removed from the cage. But that was not true for a smaller group of passive mice that were allowed to exercise for several weeks. The fit passive mice, though submissive toward their more aggressive cagemate, recovered well when taken out of the combative situation. This smaller subgroup of passive mice seemed stress-resistant. These mice had developed resilience—because they were allowed to exercise and release stress and gain all the other mental and physical benefits physical activity brings.[1]

Not only are resilient people healthier, but health is also sustained by a resilient attitude. Those who are resilient in the face of adversity have a sense that they have some ability to *act in an effective way*. The most stressful events—this should come as no surprise—are those that come unexpectedly and feel as if they are outside of one's control. One of the hallmarks of resilient people is the ability to feel that there is something they can do about their circumstances. We may not be able to wish away, or even survive, let's say, heart disease, but if we feel that we can actively do something to make life better despite illness, then we may be more likely to live longer, with fewer complications, and have a better chance of long-term recovery.

Take Stock

Let's evaluate where you are with your health. Circle yes or no.

Do you consider yourself a healthy person?   YES NO

Do you feel good about your body?   YES NO

Do you have consistent energy throughout
the day?   YES NO

Do you make healthful dietary choices
overall?   YES NO

If you are on a diet, is it unrestrictive enough
that it remains a positive experience?   YES NO

Do you focus on eating wholesome, colorful,
balanced meals?   YES NO

Do you feel strong and capable?   YES NO

Do you engage in some type of activity every
day for at least forty-five minutes?   YES NO

Are you currently a nonsmoker?   YES NO

Are you eating enough variety of colorful
fruits, vegetables, and whole grains?   YES NO

If you have mostly yes answers, then you're doing well. If mostly no, it's important to make strides to improve your health. In fact, we all can do a bit more to improve our health and support resilience wherever we currently are on the spectrum. Reach out to the right professionals for guidance such as nutritionists, physical trainers, and others, if you feel that you need help in a certain area.

Daily Dos

....

Morning: Using the Take Stock inventory above as a starting point for reference, write down general areas that need improvement (exercise, nutrition, relaxation, sleep, etc.) at the top of a new page. Now that you have identified general areas, break them down into more manageable, very specific tasks. For example, if nutrition is an area that needs to improve, more specific tasks include eating more nuts and beans, red meat once per month, limiting fried food to only occasionally. Next, create a timeline in your current calendar. To continue the example, the timeline might include these notes: "Next week, I will eat more whole grains in at least one meal per day (and I'll write it into my calendar as a reminder). First Sunday of the month is my red meat day. Tuesday and Thursday I will have fish one meal per day." Now you're equipped to make real change, and it's not just a vague goal.

Day: Stop quantifying health. Being healthy is not about counting calories, weighing ourselves, adding up meals, or tracking workouts. For many of us, stepping on a scale, for example, has the power to completely transform how we feel. Whatever numbers appear on the display inevitably change our emotion, our perspective, and our outlook. Quantifying our health does not provide positive results. Making lifestyle changes does. The restrictive and statistic-based approach that is often advocated actually works *against* our neurological wiring. It's harder for our brain to help us accomplish our goals when we are constantly worrying about every morsel we eat and how much we're exercising. When you have an accepting, positive approach to health, you will reap the benefits.

Night: Are you on a diet? If you are, I'm going to take the bold move of asking you to stop it. Tonight is the last of your diet. Forget about "diet" in the normal sense of the word. Setting arbitrary standards, restricting specific foods, or worse yet, avoiding entire food groups are all bad ideas. First, these changes can result in nutritional deficiencies and slower metabolic processes, both of which cause weight gain. Second, restriction has been shown in studies to set us up to fail, mostly because it works against how our brains are wired. A study published a few years ago in the journal *Appetite* demonstrated how, when restricted from eating carbs for three days, women binged—eating a whopping 44 percent more than usual—when carbs were allowed back in their diet. Traditional "dieting," which requires calorie counting, restriction, and firm rules of what to eat and what not to eat, simply doesn't work long term. Instead make your "diet" or what you eat consist of *choices*, not restrictions. I focus on what I elect to do—what foods I want to eat that are healthy, and how those foods support my goals and make me feel good. Psychologically, focusing on having choices puts your brain back in control. It's a highly effective technique because it is empowering; it teaches your brain that the choices you make directly affect whether your mind and body feel good. Essentially, it primes your brain to be driven by cause and effect.

Lifelong: Every time you feel yourself saying "I should . . ." as in "I should go to yoga" or "I should order a salad," reframe it as an "I want" statement, as in "I want to get my body moving to release some energy" or "I want to feel light and not bloated this afternoon," so it's more effective. This will help you stay on track with your goals and won't feel like a nagging, negative behavior that you do motivated by guilt. Once you've created your "want," goal-oriented statement, schedule in your calendar an action to achieve it. So "I want to get my body moving to release some energy" becomes "I'll go for a power walk in the neighborhood at 7:00 tonight after work." This way you'll start to connect goals with actions. You'll learn over time to reframe passive thoughts and comments into proactive behaviors to support your growing resilience.

Control

....

My life didn't please me, so I created my life.

COCO CHANEL

Resilient people believe that what they choose to do will directly affect the outcome of a situation. Resilience depends on this control—we have a part to play in the resolution of a challenge. Otherwise we'd behave aimlessly. Control makes us feel as if we have the power to select how certain aspects of our lives unfold, which can be deeply calming and rewarding. Making active choices literally reduces stress and increases our happiness-inducing hormone called dopamine.[1] Resilience lies in being able to get in touch with feelings of control, and exercise mastery, without letting oneself be limited by overregulation. It requires being able to adapt as things change while still making choices that reinforce goals and integrity. It's a tough line to straddle, but resilient people are able to do it well (see chapter 12 on flexibility).

"Learned helplessness" is a term psychologists came up with to describe what happens when people feel as if they have no control over their environment. This is what resilient people do *not* feel. When we become convinced that our actions will not have the impact we want (or any impact at all), we become helpless and passive. We don't take any actions to change how we feel or what our lives are like—even if we know better and are capable of making the change we so desperately seek.

What's crucial to understand is that biology and circumstances are not our destiny—we can actually control and affect our outcomes. Take one of my favorite experiments of all time: In 1979, Dr. Ellen Langer, a professor of psychology at Harvard University, conducted a study in which a group of male nursing home residents in their late seventies and early eighties went on a week-long retreat that re-created for them what it was like in 1959, twenty years earlier.[2] Everything about their retreat was a blast from the past—they saw magazines, newspapers, films, TV and radio programs dated from that year, and they participated in discussions about events that occurred that year and the work they had been doing then as though it were the present. What happened? They literally became younger. The study showed improvement in flexibility, height, weight, posture, and even finger length as their arthritis diminished. And they even looked younger based on unbiased observers.

This experiment illustrates just how much power and control we have even over something as intrinsically biological as aging. Of course, we can't stop the inevitability of aging. But we can exert some level of control over its symptoms by being proactive in staying physically fit and healthy and by approaching the aging process in a positive way; by behaving as a youthful person with much life left instead of succumbing to our age.

Even though we might have all the latest research and information on resilience, we won't make any changes if we believe that we don't have control over those elements in our life—and because of that, we don't think that it's possible to get the outcome we want. Worse yet, we'll beat ourselves up about not being able to change.

A study published in 2012 that surveyed more than thirty years of neurological research at the University of Iowa, found that our brain uses one network to make choices and exert control and an entirely different network to guide our behavior.[3] Both networks have to be functioning well to make good choices that support resilience. When we struggle, there's a disconnect somewhere between those networks. By engaging in the techniques I discuss in the following pages, we can reset those critical neural networks and train our brain to exert control. This will help us value long-term success over immediate reward.

Control can become unhealthy when people are too controlled, or too controlling of others. Too much control will get in the way of building resilience, since resilient people are able to make effective choices but are also flexible and able to adjust well to change. We all have moments of doubt and fear and react to try to control the outcome in a way that isn't productive. How do you know how much control is healthy? Think about whether you are able to freely be yourself, both alone and also in front of others. Are you particularly hard on yourself? Do you get very upset when things don't go your way? Do you have frequent temper outbursts? Do you expect your needs to be met? Do you believe you know how other people think even if you don't? Can you accept when others say no to you, and do you have trouble making mutual decisions? These are all red flags. Seek the guidance of a mental health professional to guide you on how to exert a healthy amount of control in your life.

Take Stock

Let's take a moment to evaluate our level of control. Answer the following questions honestly:

Why do you feel like you (circle one) are/aren't in control of your life?

_____

_____

_____

_____

_____

What changes would you like to make so you can be (circle one) more/less in control?

_____

_____

_____

_____

_____

Do you think life is very much about the inevitable just happening, or do you have a say in your destiny?

_____

_____

_____

_____

_____

Daily Dos

Morning: Set an intention for the day first thing in the morning. It can be something simple like "I'm going to finish my project by the end of the day" or something more complex or challenging such as "I intend to be more giving." Set this intention and let it lead your way that day. So when you take a towel to wipe off sweat at the gym and others are waiting to get a towel behind you, remind yourself of your intention and choose to hand out some towels to people behind you to practice being more giving. This will give you a sense of completion and pride. This is a simple way to "reset" those neural networks I mentioned, the ones that help us exert control and guide behavior. When you set a goal and remind yourself of that goal every time you are faced with a choice, you are training yourself to be more in control of your life.

Day: All of us have moments when we act in a controlling way, even if we don't act that way all the time. For example, your husband says he's going out to dinner to celebrate a friend's birthday and that he'll be home late. You follow up by telling him he really shouldn't be out late because he has work the next morning. You probably mean it to be helpful, but ultimately it's controlling. Or you track your teenage daughter's cell phone without her knowing. It's a safety precaution, but it's also controlling. It is critical to be aware of your behavior and have enough emotional intelligence (see chapter 16) to recognize this. When you feel yourself being controlling or getting upset when things don't go your way, take a deep breath. Realize what's happening in that moment, and let it go. When choosing to give up control comes from this kind of self-awareness, it's more lasting and reinforces resilience.

Night: Identify a behavior you want to change. Make note of why you want to change it and how it negatively affects others. Now list three ways by which you can change it. For example, if you feel like you nag your kids, here are three ways to change: (1) When you find yourself about to say something that might be nagging, stop and think instead. (2) Is the comment necessary to say at that moment? If it is, how can you say it in a way that's constructive? If not, when is a good time to bring it up later to make more of an impact? Or is it something you don't even need to say? (3) What behaviors in your kids make you feel like you need to nag? Is there a pattern? Work on figuring out what triggers the nagging so you can be attuned and give commentary in a more effective way.

Lifelong: Imagine an outcome you want in your life. Do you want to have a family but are single right now? Are you in an unhappy marriage and scared to be alone? Do you spend too much time working and not enough time living? Write it down, whatever it may be. Now figure out what is needed to get to that outcome by creating steps to achieve it. Identify no more than ten steps, and make sure they're all manageable. By making calculated decisions, you are crafting a nearly infallible way of obtaining that goal methodically. Just make sure you're able to "go with the flow" if things get sidetracked.

Day 5

Playfulness

....

To truly laugh you must be able to take your pain
and play with it.

CHARLIE CHAPLIN

I used to run group therapy meetings at an in-patient drug rehab facility when I was in college. I noticed people made the most progress during meetings when there was humor infused in our conversation. When patients poked fun at themselves, they were acknowledging their addiction and pain in a light-hearted way that allowed them to move forward. The humor broke the intensity and weightiness of the conversation, and in turn it provided room for extra support and encouragement. Humor was a valuable tool that helped patients heal.

It's probably not news to you that playfulness is good for our social, emotional, physical, and cognitive health, which supports our resilience. It is a diversion that pulls us out of the immediate emotion and allows us space to move forward. Humor promotes objectivity, which is essential in generating resilience. It also creates a domino effect and in that way increases social connectivity and trust, further strengthening our resilience muscle.

Humor is in fact innate—babies laugh from four months old, and all children use humor to entertain themselves and others. But where does that raw sense of humor go as we age? Life gets to us. We start to censor ourselves as we get older. We care too much about how people perceive us. It's unfortunate because laughter is highly therapeutic; it actually makes us happier and healthier.[1] It reduces stress hormones and allows us to release stored-up negative emotions. It strengthens our immune system and allows more time for our cells to fight disease since they're not focused on processing stress in our body. There's a myriad of benefits, but less known is that laughter is also a useful tool to build resilience.

When we are going through a difficult time, coping methods such as humor allow us to see the situation in a different way and provide relief. Do you remember the characters in Monty Python's *Life of Brian* singing "Always Look on the Bright Side of Life" as they're being crucified? Obviously an extreme example, but the irony kept such intensity light. One study showed a connection between those who had a lot of humor in their lives and those who had more positive thoughts and problem-solving strategies. People with high levels of humor in their lives also viewed themselves as having less stress and having fewer problems than those who didn't indulge in humor as often.[2] In this way humor supports resilience. This isn't to say that those of us who use humor deny the crisis or pain; in fact, it can ground us with a shifted perspective and help us pull through the darkness. But it also can't be used to avoid dealing with reality. Resilient people are able to be playful and apply humor in appropriate circumstances.

Even in the most challenging of times, people can be resilient and use humor to find peace and clarity. At my grandfather's funeral, loved ones shared a myriad of funny stories that brought his memory back to life. It was a way to come together, to face his death head-on, and also a tool to move forward. In *Man's Search for Meaning,* psychiatrist Viktor Frankl summarized it best when he wrote about surviving Nazi concentration camps: "Humor was another of the soul's weapons in the fight for self-preservation. It is well known that humor, more than anything else in the human makeup, can afford an aloofness and an ability to rise above any situation, even if only for a few seconds."[3]

Take Stock

Now it's time to evaluate your playfulness and sense of humor.

How often do you laugh?

NEVER   OCCASIONALLY   FREQUENTLY   ALWAYS

Are you the type of person who appreciates a good joke?

NEVER   OCCASIONALLY   FREQUENTLY   ALWAYS

Do you use humor to break the ice in social settings?

NEVER   OCCASIONALLY   FREQUENTLY   ALWAYS

Do you gravitate toward others who use humor in their conversations?

NEVER   OCCASIONALLY   FREQUENTLY   ALWAYS

Is humor one of the main characteristics that you look for in a partner?

NEVER   OCCASIONALLY   FREQUENTLY   ALWAYS

Do you consider yourself lighthearted?

NEVER   OCCASIONALLY   FREQUENTLY   ALWAYS

Do you find yourself reverting to humor when you feel uncomfortable?

NEVER   OCCASIONALLY   FREQUENTLY   ALWAYS

Do you seek out comedy in your life, whether it's comedy shows, funny books, movies, etc.?

NEVER   OCCASIONALLY   FREQUENTLY   ALWAYS

Do you often get feedback from others that you're funny or that they enjoy your sense of humor?

NEVER   OCCASIONALLY   FREQUENTLY   ALWAYS

Have you ever had humor get you in trouble, or have you gone too far with it?

NEVER   OCCASIONALLY   FREQUENTLY   ALWAYS

If you're on the "always" side of the spectrum, you probably already have a healthy dose of humor in your life. The reality is that, whether you're currently playful or don't have any humor in your bones, we all could use more laughter. Science has found laughter to literally be contagious both visually and auditorily. One study on the topic involving 128 participants found that *laughter itself* produces more laughter, possibly by activating a laughter-specific auditory detector in the brain.[4] What a great way to give to others—the gift of laughter. Let's explore some ways to work on increasing humor.

Daily Dos

Morning: Look back at a typical morning when something happened that was upsetting or irritating; now challenge yourself to see the lighter side of it. Life can be seen from the lens of comedy, especially if you train yourself to sometimes use a satirical perspective. For instance, yesterday I was feeding my baby a bowl of oatmeal. I walked away for a second to help my toddler with his meal, and, of course, when I turned around not only did she have the entire bowl of oatmeal on her head, but she was also trying to reach the oatmeal on her head with a spoon and eat it that way. We were in a rush to get out the door, and as irritating as it was because of the cleanup, I couldn't help but giggle. And what did I do with the box of cereal that was supposed to be placed back into the pantry? I put it in the fridge, on autopilot. Of course.

Day: Are there people in your life who don't take themselves too seriously, who you feel have a good sense of humor? Spend some time talking to and learning from them: What do they do that makes you laugh? How do they deal with situations? Do they actually tell jokes, or are they just sarcastic? Is there anything you can take away from their behavior? If you surround yourself with people who make you laugh, their good sense of humor will inevitably rub off on you.

Night: In the morning we worked on seeing the bright side in even small annoyances. Now let's dig a little deeper. Think about something negative that happened today that you took pretty seriously. Maybe it was a rejection letter from a school or employer, or a fight with your partner. Try to find the humor in it somehow. A client of mine once told me of a heated argument she had with her stepmom. As she was describing it to me, she was getting emotional about it all over again. I wanted help to find lightness in the situation, so I asked her to describe the physicality of the argument, and as she was describing how red in the face her stepmom became, she broke out laughing hysterically. Refocusing her attention on something other than the raw emotion attached to the disagreement helped her find humor in it. So for your exercise, try to put intense emotions aside (and since it's later in the day, you've probably had time to calm down) and challenge yourself to find humor in it. Was there some twist or irony to notice? Was the other person's hair sticking up? Were you spitting as you were talking? Did the spit land on the other person's face? Did you pass gas unknowingly because you were nervous? (People always find that funny for some reason!) You get the point. It's hard to do, but you can find humor in almost anything if you try.

Lifelong: Developing a sense of humor is not something we can just do on cue. We tend to take ourselves too seriously, and we need to change that. Write down below the last time you were embarrassed about something. What was particularly embarrassing about it? Is there a way in which you can shift the lens and find humor in the embarrassment to not take it so personally? Learn to loosen up and trust yourself. Trust that there is humor within you—you just need to bring it out! So relax and let it flow. This is a lifelong pursuit; you'll get there.

_____

_____

_____

_____

_____

Day 6

Self-Respect

You can search throughout the entire universe for someone who is more deserving of your love and affection than you are yourself, and that person is not to be found anywhere. You, yourself, as much as anybody in the entire universe, deserve your love and affection.

GAUTAMA BUDDHA

Resilience isn't built just by liking yourself. The type of self-confidence that is directly related to resilience equates to having respect for yourself and building that respect from positive experiences and contributions to society, rather than just one's sense of self-worth or personal value. Confidence that is infused with honor and dignity, that is grounded in reality based on one's true behavior—not confidence for the sake of feeling good or self-advancement—is what resilience is rooted in.

If confidence were a seesaw on a playground, this confidence would be sitting right in the middle, with arrogance on one end and dissatisfaction on the other! Going too far in any one direction would cause equilibrium to tip.

Resilient people have a high degree of self-worth that they have built based on the achievement of their goals. They are comfortable as themselves and respect themselves enough to have the courage to bounce back from trauma and challenges. They are strengthened by their achievements, by their respect for others, by their abilities and sustained friendships. Their behavior and experiences have taught them to deem themselves worthy enough to fight through the pain, to put in the extra effort required to persevere in the face of adversity.

Studies show a relationship between negative self-regard and risky behaviors related to drug and alcohol abuse, especially among adolescent boys.[1] It makes sense—if you don't find yourself worthy enough to take care of yourself or make healthy choices, you're more likely to engage in risky behaviors. Self-respect is a buffer against risk and stressors. In this way self-respect encourages resilience. People who are resilient are able to maintain a high sense of self-respect in spite of the challenges they endure, which protects them.

Plus, if you don't have self-respect, others around you won't either, which further depletes your sense of self-worth. It's a cyclical relationship between self-respect and resilience—if you exhibit dignity, people around you will also regard you as being worth supporting and assisting.

The key to resilient people is that they let the negative, challenging times *teach* them important lessons—they don't let those moments define them. They have enough self-respect to know they're worth the effort to persevere, and they allow their successes, however minor, to propel them through those down times.

Take Stock

We don't generally think about our level of self-respect. Here's a questionnaire for you to dig a little deeper.

Do you feel uncomfortable with praise
or compliments?   YES NO

Do you have a hard time standing up
for yourself and your opinions?   YES NO

Do you always want to please others?   YES NO

Do you care a lot about what people think
about you?   YES NO

Do you belittle yourself in your head
or even to others?   YES NO

Do you accept being treated poorly
by those who say they love you?   YES NO

Do you often feel guilty or embarrassed
about your past?   YES NO

Do you neglect yourself or have a hard
time relaxing?   YES NO

If some of these are true for you, don't worry. These are all
things that can be improved over time, creating a self worthy
enough for respect. This will provide yet another critical tool in
your resilience tool kit.

Daily Dos

Morning: You might have heard of the mirror exercise. But
mine isn't about what you like about yourself physically. This
is a tool you're going to use while thinking about your personality, plus an added twist. The mirror is indeed a great mecha-
nism. We often look at it in passing, or if we stare for a while,
many of us are critical of what we see.

Set a timer for three minutes. This might seem like an
eternity when staring at yourself. At first you might feel very
uncomfortable. While you're looking at yourself physically,
look deeper into your eyes and think about your personality. What do you like about your personality? Think of several
things and make note in your mind. If you can't find anything
you like about yourself in that moment, that's okay. After three
minutes are up, set the timer again, for three minutes, but
now straighten your back and posture. Squeeze your shoulder
blades tightly together and then relax them slowly, but keep
that poised posture. Now look back at yourself in the mirror.
Do you notice you can name a few more things about your

personality that you like? Jot down on a piece of paper some of those qualities you appreciate. Research shows good posture actually makes you feel better about yourself and increases self-confidence.[2] Just a simple straightening of posture primes your brain to be more receptive to yourself and to feel more powerful. In fact, social psychologist Amy Cuddy suggests that not only does body posture affect our mood, but it can also change our body chemistry. Her studies show that after only two minutes of "faking" good posture, participants' stress hormones decreased, their testosterone increased, and they were more likely to take risks. How we move our bodies is directly related to how we feel and behave.[3]

Day: Let's take the activity you did in the morning a step farther. In addition to noting what you like about your personality, now focus on your potential, not your limitations. Write down what you're really good at currently and what you've been successful with in the past. Try to come up with five to ten things. It might seem like a lot, but there are many things you are good at, whether you see them at first or not. They could be related to your career, relationships, personal life, creativity, anything. Training yourself to focus on what you are capable of instead of your deficiencies is empowering, fosters self-worth, and will set you up for resilience in the future.

Night: Self-affirmations are powerful. We see it in the movie *The Help,* when nanny Aibileen Clark reminds Elizabeth Leefolt's daughter that "you is kind, you is smart, you is important," even when her own mother told her otherwise. These affirmations change her future. Pick some mantras to tell yourself in the evening several times over and over. It will feel very silly at first. But after a few minutes you'll start to believe it. Experts say that the power of repeated affirmations, or mantras, is in the vibrations of the words that stimulate certain parts of the brain and change its chemical balance to help us become more relaxed and more receptive to positive messaging. "I am strong," "I am beautiful," "I am humble," "I am confident"—whatever you need to hear at that moment in your life. What would you want someone else on the sidelines of your life telling you repeatedly? Now become your own coach.

Lifelong: I think we would all agree that one of the best ways to maintain self-worth throughout a lifetime is to have continued success and build on those successes. Because of this, it's important to have a long-term approach. If you see your life as only a series of failures, it's very hard to have the confidence and self-respect that resilience requires. If you're having a hard time seeing the successes in your life, start very small. It could be as simple as the fact that you were able to resist buying that bag of chips at the grocery store and instead bought fruit; or that you made it through the morning without having road rage on your way to work; or that you woke up five minutes ahead of schedule and didn't feel rushed. These minor "wins" will color your world, and it will soon become a subconscious process the more you practice this. When your brain is primed with positivity and success, more positivity and success will follow.

Day 7

Self-Awareness

....

"Self-knowledge is better than self-control any day,"
Raquel said firmly. "And I know myself well enough
to know how I act around cookies."

CLAUDIA GRAY, *Evernight*

Resilient people understand that whatever is causing their temporary pain does not define them in totality. They are discerning enough that they know it will pass. They separate the self from the sensation—and don't define themselves as their feelings. Emotions definitely shape us and are important to our identity, but they are not all of what we are. Self-awareness increases self-worth and strengthens identity,[1] which, in turn, improves our ability to bounce back from challenges.

We can classify self-awareness in three primary categories: cognitive (thoughts), emotional (feelings), and behavioral (actions). Most of us have many blind spots when it comes to knowing ourselves. We rationalize our own behavior; we get caught up in our feelings and often think we're always right. This is when our resilience plummets.

So how does self-awareness actually help us deal with problems or stress? Here's an example a client shared with me. Her husband was out late at a business dinner. She's become more self-aware over time and realized right when he told her he may be out late, she physically clamped up. When he got home, she gave him the cold shoulder and pretended she was sleeping but noticed she was pacing a bit while he was gone and ate a little more ice cream than she should have. Without judgment she was mindful of her reaction in the moment—she clamps up when she feels jealous, eats ice cream when upset, and paces when she ruminates. She realized what was happening but didn't want to talk about it when he got home late because they were both so tired, and it would only make things worse. So as they were having breakfast the next morning, she explained to him that she felt irritated that he was out late because they haven't spent a lot of time together lately. She was jealous of his coworkers. They realized that date nights needed to be a priority. He responded positively, and they went out together a few nights later, totally reconnecting.

Now, this could have been a very different situation had it been someone who wasn't as self-aware. It could have led to a blow-up fight that lasted weeks if she had been confrontational and accusatory, followed by intense anger and hurt feelings from mean things he might have said to defend himself. There likely wouldn't have been any resolution, so the same issue would come up again, causing many fights like this as well as accumulated feelings of distance, resentment, jealousy, and disdain from having a destructive communication style, and the marriage could very easily have ended in divorce down the road. To be sure, this is taking a pretty common conflict to its worst-case scenario, but it's easy to see how self-awareness can really make that much of a difference, especially when it comes to dealing with stress and bouncing back from challenges.

One of the best ways we can get to know our true selves is through paying attention, with curiosity rather than judgment, to our current experience. Nonjudgmental concern not only helps us understand our emotional and cognitive self better, but also helps us become more aware of our physical body and behavior. For example, when I get nervous I feel a little queasy. This physical response to my emotions serves as a cue and gives me more insight. People often get red in the face when they're embarrassed—blushing is another physical reaction to a psychological emotion. By knowing more about yourself, you will also be able to manage your behavior and avoid reacting too quickly based solely on emotions. This can save you from behaving in ways that you wouldn't feel proud of. By becoming more self-aware, you are becoming more resilient.

Take Stock

Do you feel as if you have a good sense of your likes and dislikes? What are they?

Likes: _____

Dislikes: _____

Do you often run into people who tell you something about yourself that you're surprised to learn about? What surprised you recently about yourself?

_____

_____

_____

_____

_____

How and when do you find yourself getting stuck in your feelings?

_____

_____

_____

_____

_____

Do you have a sense of what you can do to make yourself feel better when you're in a funk? Write some ideas down here:

_____

_____

_____

_____

_____

What are your physical reactions to certain feelings?

Feeling: anger
Physical reaction:_____

Feeling: fear
Physical reaction:_____

Feeling: joy
Physical reaction:_____

Feeling: sadness
Physical reaction:_____

Feeling: love
Physical reaction:_____

Feeling: pride
Physical reaction:_____

Feeling: embarrassment
Physical reaction:_____

Feeling: hurt
Physical reaction:_____

Feeling: excitement
Physical reaction:_____

Feeling: disgust
Physical reaction:_____

Daily Dos

Morning: Resilient people are aware of themselves and their environment at any given moment. Let's practice. There are a lot of questions you can ask yourself, and you can spend as much time as you want. The key here is to keep it simple and succinct at first as you get used to this process.

What emotions am I feeling right now?

_____

_____

_____

_____

What sensations am I experiencing in my body?

_____

_____

_____

_____

What am I doing physically at this moment?

_____

_____

_____

_____

And then, if you want to connect the dots and take it deeper: What are my emotions revealing about what I'm doing right now? What are my bodily sensations telling me?

_____

_____

_____

_____

_____

Day: Awareness has to do with focus. Our days can get frenzied with external stimuli; it's important to know how to regain our attention so we can better attune to our surroundings, and to ourselves. Here's my trick to improve focus: Any time you want to tune in better, rub your index finger on your thumb for a few seconds. Stare at it, and focus on the sensation it produces. Do this with each finger on your hand for a second or two. Try it now. This will help you snap back into attention, and integrate physical sensation with behavior and feelings. Now get back to the task at hand, and see what a difference it makes.

Night: Learning more about your needs and how to better take care of yourself increases self-awareness. Try this cognitive exercise to get better at it.

Are you at your best when you're active or sedentary?

_____

Do you enjoy being around friends, or are you happier being solitary? _____

Write below what calms you, what makes you happy, what gives you peace and serenity.

_____

_____

_____

_____

_____

Every day, look through this list and make sure you've done at least one thing that makes you feel good today. By taking care of yourself, you will improve your mental health, increase positive feelings, and ultimately support the process of building resilience.

Lifelong: Self-awareness needs to be consistent and non-judgmental for it to be effective. Pay attention to how stimulated you are throughout the day during various tasks. Are you generally bored, just right, or overwhelmed? Noticing how you function will help you pinpoint problem areas where you can make adjustments in what you do and _how_ you do things. Over time you will be able to figure out what your emotions and body are actually telling you—what insights are they giving you? Your emotions, behaviors, and thoughts are the best clues you have into how you can most effectively rebound from any stressful or traumatic event. Self-awareness is one of the best tools you can use to build resilience.

Week 2

SPIRIT

Realistic Optimism

....

Don't cry because it's over, smile because it happened.

DR. SEUSS

Optimism is resilience's fuel. Without an optimistic outlook, we can't bounce back from trauma and learn from challenges. Without the expectation of a positive outcome, you're less likely to push through difficulty. Optimists also are more likely to be multi-dimensional in their response to dealing with distress and thus will consider more options when coping with difficult situations—which is a fundamental characteristic of problem solving related to resilience.[1] Science has repeatedly proven that people who are optimistic generally are more protective of themselves, are successful, are more lively and spirited, and have better physical health, all of which further support resilience.[2]

Look at optimism like an eyeglass prescription. Some people have perfect vision and see the world completely balanced, 20/20; others need corrective lenses. Some are a little too pessimistic; some can be unrealistically optimistic. The key is to learn what prescription you need and adjust accordingly.

Where we are naturally on the optimism scale is partly due to our genes. We are not born as "blank slates"; our brains are extremely malleable. There are different genes and chemical systems within our bodies that predispose us to pay more attention to the good or to the bad in our environment. But that's just a tendency—not our destiny. In other words, we can teach our brain how we want it to react to the world around us.

Every single outcome in our lives improves once we begin to think positively about our present and our future, including our resilience. The reason why is simple: our expectations prime our behavior. If we expect positive outcomes, we are more likely to make choices that support those outcomes. For example, suppose you've recently gone through a divorce, and even though the pain is real, you expect to find happiness again; you almost certainly will because you will make choices moving forward that lead you toward your expectations. It's just the way we are psychologically wired. However, if we expect to be unhappy, if we expect that we won't find a loving partner again, we are less likely to care about the choices we make and we accept defeat—because we expect it. Unhappiness comes as no surprise so we don't fight against it. We don't have a reason to if we welcome it. So it's true that optimism and pessimism can be somewhat prophetic. They're clues into our future and are self-fulfilling. Change your outlook and you'll slowly start to change the lens with which you see the world, changing your behavior and outcomes as a result.

I stress "realistic optimism" because it's important that our optimism be tempered by realistic thinking. Every day doesn't have to be happy and cheery—that's not what optimism is about. That kind of unrealistic outlook is just a veil to hide deeper issues. It's the kind of bubbly, pernicious happiness that reeks of being false.

Optimism that's authentic is consistent over time. In this way, happiness becomes a state of being, not feeling euphoria. This type of realistic optimism supports the understanding that no matter what happens, you are content with your life. You know that what good and bad comes is transitory; you don't let those moments define you. That's what drives resilience.

People who are resilient are okay with sitting in the negative, feeling real sadness, experiencing the gamut of emotions. Truly resilient people know that a huge part of the process is accepting the bad feelings that come with adversity, not trying to escape them. You experience them, learn from them, and fight back. You grow from them. They strengthen you. You realize that avoidance and fear are weaknesses. You embrace the negative and let it empower you to persevere. You have figured out how to make weaknesses into strengths. Resilient people are optimistic while also accepting their range of emotions.

It's extraordinary to see how optimism and resilience can triumph over the most horrendous of circumstances, even when all hope may have evaporated. Etty Hillesum was a courageous woman living during the Holocaust. In her diary from that time period, she wrote about hope, that she loved her life even amid such horror.[3] In an entry after being verbally assaulted by Gestapo agents, she wrote, "I am not easily frightened. Not because I am brave but because I know that I am dealing with human beings and that I must try as hard as I can to understand everything that anyone ever does. And that was the real import of this morning: not that a disgruntled young Gestapo officer yelled at me, but that I felt no indignation, rather a real compassion, and would have liked to ask, 'Did you have a very unhappy childhood, has your girlfriend let you down?'" She writes of the horrors she and her loved ones endured with eyes wide open, while also maintaining unwavering optimism and resilience. She wrote, "I know and share the many sorrows a human being can experience, but I do not cling to them; they pass through me, like life itself, as a broad eternal stream . . . and life continues." The only way she was able to cope was to find a sense of peace within herself, to be able to endure. "Ultimately, we have just one moral duty: to reclaim large areas of peace in ourselves, more and more peace, and to reflect it toward others. And the more peace there is in us, the more peace there will also be in our troubled world." She fought hard to maintain her resilience and hope—until she died at Auschwitz in 1943.

What differentiates resilient optimists from others is the level of reality they are able to adjust for, and their self-efficacy (belief in one's own abilities). We see this clearly in studies with cancer patients. The worst outcomes are for those with a pessimistic attitude who feel defeated by the disease. The body listens to what the mind says, so when we give up mentally, this affects our physical state, which seems to give up, too. Optimists, on the other hand, generally have better outcomes. It's not a ticket to definitive survival, but it definitely increases one's chances. Since optimistic cancer patients believe they will survive, this positive attitude primes their body to endure so they make behavioral and treatment choices to support this vitality. Realistic optimists do even better. They are able to accept their current situation and that they don't know what the future holds, while also fighting to survive. That's where the self-efficacy comes in. Patients who are able to accept unpredictability, while simultaneously taking an active role in recovery and remaining optimistic, have a greater likelihood of long-term flourishing.[4] Cancer patient or not, this applies to everyone in life.

Take Stock

Take a short quiz to see where you are with realistic optimism.

It doesn't take me long to shake off a bad mood.

STRONGLY AGREE/AGREE/DISAGREE/STRONGLY DISAGREE

I set realistic, challenging goals to strive toward.

NEVER/OCCASIONALLY/FREQUENTLY/ALWAYS

I believe in the saying "Where there's a will, there's a way."

STRONGLY AGREE/AGREE/DISAGREE/STRONGLY DISAGREE

I'm generally confident before an interview.

NEVER/OCCASIONALLY/FREQUENTLY/ALWAYS

I rely on my own sensibility when making decisions.

NEVER/OCCASIONALLY/FREQUENTLY/ALWAYS

The glass is always half full.

NEVER/OCCASIONALLY/FREQUENTLY/ALWAYS

No matter what challenge I'm confronted with, I feel that after all is said and done, I will be okay.

STRONGLY AGREE/AGREE/DISAGREE/STRONGLY DISAGREE

I'll be pleased when I lose those extra five pounds, but my happiness doesn't depend on it.

STRONGLY AGREE/AGREE/DISAGREE/STRONGLY DISAGREE

Life isn't always great; I've been through tough times, but I persevere.

STRONGLY AGREE/AGREE/DISAGREE/STRONGLY DISAGREE

I'm generally pleased with my life, even with the challenges I've been through.

STRONGLY AGREE/AGREE/DISAGREE/STRONGLY DISAGREE

If you've answered on the left side of the spectrum for most of the questions, you have a good handle on optimism. If most of your answers were on the right side, you have to work on building it. We all can. Here's how.

Daily Dos

Morning: Perfectionism is an interesting trait that many of us exhibit. It's further amplified by our culture's focus on flawlessness. There are some arguments in favor of perfectionistic tendencies, saying that it produces true greatness. But more often than not, this quest to be the very best gets in the way of our success. Why? It leaves too large of a window for failure and keeps us focused on what's wrong, as opposed to what's right. It gets in the way of optimism, which is crucial to resilience and well-being. Here's an exercise supported by neuroscience that you can do to counteract our tendency toward perfectionism, in turn increasing optimism: wake up with this mantra—good enough is good enough. Research shows that trying to be the best is much too stressful for our brain and actually impedes our decision-making capabilities.[5] Remind yourself every morning that things might not be perfect and go your way. This is important to setting yourself up for realistic optimism since it puts the power directly in your hands. You're less likely to become unglued when life gets sidetracked. You won't waste precious energy on yearning for unrealistic outcomes and rather spend that energy on problem solving and getting back on track.

Day: Fake it. It really works. Your brain can actually be tricked into feeling happier. Studies have shown that something as simple as smiling when you're sad, chemically increases happiness—it triggers a part of your brain that actually makes you feel more jovial and optimistic.[6] It will feel strange at first, but slowly you'll feel a lightness, a little joy creep in—the boost you need to persevere. The same goes for other simple adjustments: Research has shown that how we position our body sends direct messages to our brain about how we should feel. Sitting a little straighter or holding your head high will make you feel more confident and have a greater sense of well-being,[7] which will encourage optimism since a greater sense of well-being and confidence is a precursor to having a positive attitude toward the future. Plus, our brains are wired to be social. So if we see another person smile, neurons will activate as if we were smiling ourselves, increasing positive feelings and building optimism. What better thing to be contagious than happiness!

Night: What objects in your environment or common behavior have a negative effect on your mind-set? Observe, note, and then make appropriate changes that support the positive outlook you are trying to achieve. We do many things automatically but don't stop and think how that affects us. Be mindful and proactive. For example, I noticed that watching more than one news broadcast in a day negatively influenced my outlook, so I limited myself to only fifteen minutes of viewing or none at all. Now I skim over the newspaper or a synopsis of the day's events online.

Lifelong: You are what you say. Words have great power, so use them accordingly. Notice your words and change your vocabulary. Start writing down your feelings about events that have transpired and make note of the words you use to describe them. Are they mostly negative? Is there a mix? This will take some time, but it will help you see how you perceive and also receive the world. Eventually you can change the narrative. When something happens at work, instead of thinking the worst—"I messed up. I always mess up. I'm not good at this job. He'll find someone else to replace me. I'm a failure."—you will be able to reword it. You could say, "I messed up" (you can still acknowledge failure—that's healthy, but making a general statement about how you always do something negative is debilitating and creates hopelessness, not hopefulness), and "This doesn't feel good" (you can still admit the negative feelings it creates—now reframe with a positive lens), and "I will learn from this and do better next time." It's a simple shift, but it will change your outcome.

Mindfulness

···

Be happy in the moment, that's enough.
Each moment is all we need, not more.

MOTHER TERESA

I was on the trip of a lifetime. My husband, Joel, and I had just arrived on the Big Island of Hawaii for a rare two-week vacation (this was before we had kids). On our second day there, we were riding our bikes to a beautiful, secluded beach. En route we hit some dicey terrain, and with unexpected strong wind gusts coming off the volcano, I was thrown from my bike as I made the descent off the last hill. By the time Joel ran over to me, the contusion on my face was the size of a large grapefruit. He had never seen anything like it, and coming from an athlete who played a variety of contact sports, that says a lot. There was gravel embedded in my skin from head to toe, and the pain throughout my body, especially my left arm, was almost paralyzing. I had to get to a hospital—but wouldn't you know it, in an attempt to unplug, we had left our phones behind. And we were pretty far off the beaten path, so there wasn't much traffic on the roads. By pure luck (and perhaps some other type of divine intervention), a car appeared. The woman driving graciously came to our aid. She wrapped me in the towels she had in her trunk and held me tight as we drove toward help. I will never forget what she said. She whispered in my ear, "Embrace the pain. Embrace the moment. You are stronger than you ever know. Breathe—one-two-three. Just like that. Breathe into the pain. Embrace the pain. You are stronger than you ever know. We are here now. Be here now." It became a mantra, a chant, repeating those words over and over again to prevent me from falling unconscious.

I took a long time to heal and will forever have titanium screws in my arm, but I'm so grateful to say that everything turned out okay in the end. From this, I learned that mindfulness was literally the key to my resilience that day. By focusing on my breathing and by being in that moment with her, feeling the wind on my ripped skin, feeling the pain in my body—by being mindful—I was able to stay with it, not lose consciousness, and focus on what was important in my recovery. At the hospital, I was able to explain exactly what happened and even reminded the doctor to get the gravel out of my skin. With each breath, I became more aware, focused, and connected. Of course, this is a very extreme example, but the experience showed mindfulness operating at its very best, and being able to apply it in a time of such crisis was particularly powerful and telling. Research in fact has shown mindfulness to be a key element in reducing the posttraumatic effects of suffering.[1] Plus, the more stressed we are, the more we need it. A study from the University of Washington found that your ability to multi-task and handle stress increases dramatically if you practice meditation for just eight weeks.[2]

Paying attention with purpose, without blame, is the type of mindfulness related to resilience. This type of focus and connection helps us deal with challenges more calmly and effectively. It also helps us find meaning in the mundane or even more debilitating experiences, which is critical to growing with resilience. When we are mindful of the takeaways from stressful circumstances, negative aftershocks we might otherwise experience from the hardship are greatly reduced.[3]

We mistakenly think that if we're in a meditative mode, we're not "doing" anything, that the messier our mind is, the busier we are and feel, the more we're getting done. The reality is that this type of behavior actually makes us more anxious and less likely to get things done efficiently. When we notice and embrace how busy we feel in that moment, we gift ourselves that moment to slow down. Being present literally frees us to have more room for action, flexibility, and ingenuity—and to ultimately be more resilient. Research shows that people who practiced mindfulness for even five minutes a day over three weeks reduced stress, increased life satisfaction, had better relationships with others, and felt more in control of their life.[4] Five minutes—that's all it took. Mindfulness meditations positively change our actual brain and immune function, so chemically, they strengthen our resilience as well.[5] When we learn to be present in the moment, to accept what we're feeling, good or bad, we are able to be more in control of our reactions, which is a large part of becoming more resilient.

Take Stock

How mindful are you? Let's do a written exploration to find out.

When you feel overextended, exhausted, rushed, or busy—what's your first reaction? Is this reaction something you're proud of and want to keep doing, or do you want to change? If you want to change, what do you think is a better way for you to cope?

_____

_____

_____

_____

_____

_____

Are you the type of person who half-listens to people when they're talking, or are you a good listener? Describe how you perceive yourself, and note the feedback you've received from others about this skill.

_____

_____

When you're out for a walk, are you constantly checking social media, or are you on a phone call? Describe. Is this something you want to change, and if so, how?

Do you always think about what you're doing next instead of enjoying what you're doing in the moment?

NEVER/OCCASIONALLY/FREQUENTLY/ALWAYS

Are you the type of person who does a lot of things at one time—reading e-mails, checking social media on your phone, writing a report for work, listening to music on headphones?

NEVER/OCCASIONALLY/FREQUENTLY/ALWAYS

Does the word "meditation" scare you? If so, why?

_____

_____

_____

Either way, I'm here to help. Let's get started.

Daily Dos

Morning: Instead of waking up and forcing a moment of mindfulness, give your mind permission to wander. We're constantly thinking about the things we have to do or operating within a certain framework. It's constricting, and while important, it can also be exhausting. Giving yourself an opportunity to cognitively meander is very freeing. It supports our ability to be mindful. Let yourself go wherever your mind takes you, even just for a moment. If you're having a hard time with this, open your eyes and just do nothing. Simply pay attention to what's happening, how your curtains are blowing, or the feeling of the sheets or shower on your skin. This isn't a "meditation" per se—think of it rather as an activity. You're being active within the moment, allowing your moment to take whatever shape it wants. You will see over time how much more productive, efficient, and resilient you will become when you adopt this daily practice.

Day: We all feel stress during the day at some point, some more often than others. Being mindful and resilient requires us to _feel_ the feeling. Don't just get in fight-or-flight mode and try to avoid the real issues. Just when it can't get any worse, experience the emotion of that moment, and then do one of my favorite breathing techniques; it will help you in any stressful time, I guarantee. Breathe in through your nose for the count of 4, hold for 4, and breathe out through your mouth for the count of 4. Now breathe in through your nose for the count of 3, hold for 3, and breathe out through your mouth for the count of 3. Breathe in through your nose for the count of 2, hold for 2, and breathe out through your mouth for the count of 2. Breathe in through your nose for the count of 1, hold for 1, and breathe out through your mouth for the count of 1. This will help slow heart rate and get you to refocus your energy to where it really matters. Simple, quick, and effective.

Night: One day when I drove home from work, I parked in my driveway. Or I thought it was my driveway. I looked up, and I realized I parked in front of my old house. We had moved two weeks prior, but I was so in my head, so much on autopilot, that I didn't even realize I was going the wrong way. How could I have been so oblivious? We often are inattentive, believe it or not. How many times have you smeared something on your sandwich and later discovered you put peanut butter on your turkey sub? (Okay, maybe I'm alone here, but it has happened!) The reality is that most of our daily behaviors are done out of habit. So the next time you're driving home from work or somewhere else, take this chance to notice things. Turn off the music and get off the phone (this will be hard). Notice how you feel. Notice the person next to you. Notice what your car smells like. This is something you can do with any automatic activity, such as taking a shower, eating breakfast, anything. Train yourself to notice more, and it'll do wonders for your health and well-being.

Lifelong: Our brain responds better to momentary mindfulness, not long periods. While the goal is to integrate mindfulness into your life long-term to strengthen resilience, it's impossible to always be mindful. And in fact, constant mindfulness would not be entirely beneficial. Starting with even a few minutes a day is great and can have a significant effect; slowly work up to fifteen to twenty minutes max. Your task is to take mindfulness breaks throughout the day. To do this, set the alarm on your phone to three random times per day that alert you to stop whatever you are doing. Each time the alarm rings, take some deep breaths and notice whatever you are doing for two to three minutes. Use your alarm as a cue to shift your brain to a state of awareness. Make sure to change those three times every week to make sure you don't shift to autopilot. Eventually you won't need to set an alarm, and you will become more mindful without needing to think too much about it. This is a great way to train yourself to focus on the present.

Day 10

Integrity

··

*They're certainly entitled to think that, and
they're entitled to full respect for their opinions . . .
but before I can live with other folks I've got to live
with myself. The one thing that doesn't abide by
majority rule is a person's conscience.*

HARPER LEE, *To Kill a Mockingbird*

Success will come and go, but you have to live with yourself,
and your legacy endures through the ages. We have a way of
tricking ourselves that all our actions are justified, even if they
don't align with what we think is right. We cut in line because
we're late to a meeting; that's the justification. But is it the right
thing to do? And what about all those other people waiting
patiently? Maybe they're late, too. We sneak a brownie from a
colleague's desk, hoping no one notices. But we know we took
one! We drive over the speed limit because everyone else is,

too, so we're actually going with the speed of traffic, and there are no police around, so it doesn't matter, right? We've all been there. This constant internal justification can be exhausting and ultimately self-sabotaging. Acting in a way that puts you at odds with your values can be a far greater punishment than anything else in your life. Guilt, regret, shame, humiliation, remorse are as damaging, if not more, than feelings that arise from trauma such as fear and pain. Living a life with honor and integrity, with a sound moral compass, can give a person a lot of power—and is at the cornerstone of resilience. This strength that moral virtue provides supports people in times of trouble, helping them endure suffering and ultimately rebound even more empowered and secure.

In a *Diary of a Young Girl*, Anne Frank reminds us that "a quiet conscience makes one strong!"[1] How true. When you live your life in a way that makes you proud, no one and not any kind of pain can take away that feeling of strength and satisfaction. In this way, your general sense of contentment and purpose endures and carries you through other challenges that might arise.

If you live with regret, you can't function at your optimal capacity because regret takes up so much of your energy. You can't thrive and be fully resilient. Resilient people have consistency of character that is noticeable and palpable. Most of us have either read or seen *To Kill a Mockingbird* . . . you know the scene when Atticus goes to visit Jim's house and Jim threatens him and spits in his face but Atticus only wipes it off? He doesn't cause a scene. His son is watching from the car.

He has to behave with integrity. It's the type of honor we feel in our bones. When character is strong and unwavering, it gives you an incredible feeling of courage, almost a sense of fearlessness that is invaluable in times of stress.

When you live with integrity, life is simpler and less troublesome because you are living by your own code of conduct, and you can focus your energy on what matters rather than trying to figure out how to feel good about your choices. You don't live every day with regret that eats away at you.

Integrity and resilience have a lot to do with consistency and being dependable. When you're consistent and dependable, people learn that they can rely on you. They turn to you to help them, to solve problems, to connect. That in turn increases your self-worth, strengthens relationships, hones emotional intelligence, heightens positive emotions since you're receiving constructive reinforcement, and increases altruism since you're given more opportunities to help others when they turn to you in a crisis. When you live life with integrity, consistently and honestly, all the other elements that also build resilience inevitably are also strengthened.

A side note: People often erroneously use the words "morality" and "integrity" interchangeably, as if they're referring to the same thing. They're different. Morality is living by a certain code that you've set for yourself that usually is inspired by religion or culture; it's being able to differentiate between right and wrong (however they are defined for you) and good and bad. Morals differ among various cultures, but many are shared, since they all ultimately derive from basic human emotions. While having a moral compass is certainly of utmost importance, integrity is at its core; it is about living a life of honesty, to yourself and others, in a way that completes you and is a more internal pursuit.

Take Stock

Integrity is definitely not something you build overnight, but there are ways you can become more aware of your shortcomings and work on them over time. The first step is to see where you are with this virtue: The good news is that integrity is something we can continually upgrade and fine-tune.

Here's how.

First, answer these questions honestly:

Do you choose to do what's right more than choosing what's easy?

NEVER/OCCASIONALLY/FREQUENTLY/ALWAYS

Do you feel as if you have a moral code that drives your actions?

NEVER/OCCASIONALLY/FREQUENTLY/ALWAYS

Are you an honest person?

NEVER/OCCASIONALLY/FREQUENTLY/ALWAYS

Do you keep your promises?

NEVER/OCCASIONALLY/FREQUENTLY/ALWAYS

Are you able to build trust with others by being a person who follows through on what you say you will do?

NEVER/OCCASIONALLY/FREQUENTLY/ALWAYS

Do you stick to your core values, or do your values change based on who you're around and who you want to impress?

NEVER/OCCASIONALLY/FREQUENTLY/ALWAYS

Are you consistent with how you behave and what beliefs you value?

NEVER/OCCASIONALLY/FREQUENTLY/ALWAYS

Do you stay true to your commitments, whether they be to relationships, institutions, principles, causes, promises?

NEVER/OCCASIONALLY/FREQUENTLY/ALWAYS

Now write out your answer to this question: *How truly and deeply honest were you in your answers to my questions above?*

_____

_____

_____

_____

_____

_____

_____

    If you weren't as honest as you would like to be, try answering my questions again, but this time be brutally honest. Doesn't that feel so much better? Write down what it feels like to do it again.

_____

_____

_____

_____

_____

_____

Daily Dos

Morning: We've all lied—to ourselves, to others—for a variety of reasons. Let's practice honesty this morning. It's not just about telling the truth (which is important), but also about keeping promises. Write down a few ways you were dishonest within the past week, and think about ways you can be more honest, consistent, and dependable today. Don't punish yourself for your dishonesty—rather, use it as a tool to grow and learn.

1. I was dishonest by _____
   Today I will fix this and be honest by _____

   _____

2. I was dishonest by _____
   Today I will fix this and be honest by _____

   _____

3. I was dishonest by _____
   Today I will fix this and be honest by _____

   _____

If you have a hard time with this exercise, do a little work to figure out why you feel the need to be dishonest. Deception slowly chips away at you and can be exhausting, depleting you of your energy and resilience. Ask yourself the following questions: Do you lie because you're embarrassed or you don't think people will like the true you? Do you like the true you? Do you distort the truth to avoid punishment? Is it because you feel guilty that you use deceit to cover up the negative feeling? Take some time to work through these questions for yourself and get to the root of the issue. Accept responsibility—and vow to change moving forward.

Day: Another way to live with integrity is to make sure your career or work is something that is in line with your moral code. Even if you don't have a choice over what your job is and dislike what you do at times, it shouldn't be a job that compromises your integrity. Otherwise you will feel uneasy and drained; it'll take energy away from your ability to mediate stress, and you won't be able to bounce back from challenges as effectively.[2] Do you like what you do most of the time? Are you *always* exhausted when you get home, feeling depleted, guilty, or depressed? Do you feel like something is missing day to day with the work you do? Are you proud of it? Do you get uncomfortable about sharing what you do with others? Do you tell people the truth about your job? If not, you might be in the wrong line of work. It's never too late to change course. It won't be easy, but in the end, you will reap the benefits in all areas. If you generally like what you do, but you don't like aspects of it—for example, if you like your coworkers and are satisfied with your salary but know that your boss uses questionable business practices that make you uncomfortable—it needs to be addressed. Get creative in working out solutions, whether it's talking to your boss directly about the issue or discussing it with the human resources department. There's always a way to make things better, but it takes work and you must be committed to the process.

Night: Use the evening to reflect and reinforce. What's one thing you did today with integrity? Were you particularly honest with yourself about something? Did you stand up to the office bully? Did you reach out to your boss about making changes for yourself and your colleagues? Did you resolve a conflict with a friend in a way that made you proud? Consciously be aware of something you did—write it down here—and the satisfaction you feel is your reinforcement and reward. Soon you'll have a long list to look back on whenever you're feeling unhappy or defeated.

Today I did this right, and I'm proud of myself for it:

_____

_____

_____

_____

_____

Lifelong: People with true integrity do what they feel is right effortlessly, supporting their moral code and goals. Make sure to check in with yourself consistently to make sure your behavior matches what you want it to be. Answer the following questions throughout your lifetime, since your answers will change. The important part is to check in with yourself continually. Your answers don't always have to be virtuous, but they need to be honest. The key is to stay aware.

Are you living a life you're proud of? What legacy are you leaving for yourself?

Make a habit out of weekly reflection. Every Sunday, for example, do your integrity check-in, even if it's just for five minutes. It'll remind you about what's really important for yourself and keep you on a path of constant growth and learning. Be honest with yourself, and recognize any rationalization you may be saying to yourself instead of owning up to the truth. This simple check-in will make you more aware moving forward, and you'll be able to make thoughtful decisions throughout your life that support resilience.

Day 11

Spirituality

We are not human beings on a spiritual journey.
We are spiritual beings on a human journey.

PIERRE TEILHARD DE CHARDIN

Spirituality is about finding the miracle in every moment. The most spiritual people I know, who often are also the most resilient, continually find peace, comfort, and awe in daily life, even in the bad times. I'm not suggesting we all need to mimic the Dalai Lama, but we need to get in touch with that part of ourselves to be resilient. Spirituality is our compass—it affects choices we make in the same way a navigational compass gives us direction to get to our destination. In this way spirituality influences how we react to stressful situations and how well we recover from trauma.

I have found that spirituality has given me a sense of purpose and meaning. Do you have to be religious to be spiritual?

The answer is fairly complex, and while having a religious faith definitely encourages spirituality, you don't have to be religious to be spiritual. Religion is a belief system based on doctrines, whereas spirituality is a personal belief system that does or does not include God or a house of worship. Spirituality makes us feel as if we matter, that we're part of something larger than ourselves, and gives us a way to find comfort in life, especially in the face of traumatic events—all these things increase our resilience. Having faith in something outside ourselves makes our life worth fighting for and helps us recover from trauma and stress more easily.[1] It also encourages social connections, giving and receiving love, gratitude, acting with compassion, and empathy—all of which circle back to resilience.

Studies have shown that spirituality is connected to improved physical and mental health.[1] This enhanced health, plus the fact that spirituality provides a sense of meaning to life that can be relied upon when adversity strikes,[2] contributes to increased resilience for spiritual people. A misconception I hear often about the "God benefit" is that it's not available to people who are agnostic or atheist. Secular activities such as volunteerism, social activism, community engagement, and even a yoga practice can provide spiritual benefits similar to attending church every Sunday. Let's face it, we all know people who say they're religious or who attend a house of worship regularly but who aren't spiritual or practicing what they claim to be, right? There are also many who do attend regular religious services who are very spiritual. What matters most, and where the "God benefit" truly comes from, is participating in an activity that's for the greater good, increases our sense of belonging, or that takes us out of our own head, makes us aware of our place in this universe, and reminds us that we are meaningful. Whether that's through religion or not isn't important.

Spirituality comes in many forms. It can wash over us when we forget about the end goal or release control. It can be the feeling of being one with the world and/or intimately connected with the people around us. Many people find that having a spiritual practice, or an activity that acknowledges that they are part of an organized community, whether that's a religious/spiritual organization, a hiking group, or a book club, to be sacred. For me, I'm most connected to the intangible when I'm in nature either on a hike or in the ocean, entering a house of worship, or connecting deeply with family or friends. Finding your own source of contentment and spirituality, and spending time every day connecting with that, will boost your personal resources tremendously and increase your resilience.

Take Stock

In what ways do you consider yourself to be a spiritual person? If you don't consider yourself spiritual, in what ways do you feel meaningful? It's a similar concept, yet sometimes the word "spiritual" itself frightens people, so by reframing the question, it might be easier to answer.

_____

_____

_____

_____

_____

Have you ever felt lost or not yourself, and if so, how were you able to rebound? Did spirituality play a role in your recovery, and if so, in what way or ways?

_____

_____

_____

_____

_____

How does spirituality improve your life?

_____

_____

_____

_____

_____

_____

_____

Daily Dos

....

Morning: Who you surround yourself with has a profound effect on who you are. If you want to increase your spirituality, surround yourself with those who are also spiritual, who make you think about what spirituality means to you. You will feel more spiritual connectedness, even if you don't actively talk about it with one another.

Who in your life brings out your spiritual side? In what way or ways do they do that?

_____

_____

_____

_____

_____

_____

_____

If you don't have anyone on your list, try to make a concerted effort to look for elements of spirituality in those around you. We all project some level of this quality, some more outwardly than others.

Day: Building upon your morning activity, now, in addition to surrounding yourself with spiritual people, do something that makes you feel connected—to yourself, to others, to our world. I often find that being in nature is when I feel most spiritual. Going on a hike, surrounded by Earth's magnificence, makes me feel deep gratitude for and humbled by the beauty around me. Do whatever makes you feel that way today. Is it a hike or perhaps painting? Yoga? A walk? Visiting a place of worship (this doesn't have to be a whole church service; just walking into a temple or chapel can promote feelings of spirituality)? You can also try a new hobby, return to a sport you love, spend time with good friends, or begin a new physical activity you like. You can make anything into a spiritual experience if you take the time to consciously connect to spiritual parts of yourself. We all have it within us, but it doesn't often become our focus. When it is part of your daily life, it will energize and stabilize you in a profound way.

Night: Spirituality doesn't have to be a major—or even daunting—endeavor. It has to do with tuning into yourself and the world around you. We can do this when we quiet our minds. You read a little bit about meditation in chapter 9 on mindfulness. Tonight, take a meditative moment with this affirmation: "I am." Sit somewhere quiet, or do a walking meditation, and say "I am" out loud several times, pausing for a minute or two between each affirmation. Do this every evening, or before bed, so you start to make a habit of it. Notice how you feel when you first hear "I am." It might sound strange or uncomfortable. Over time, you can transition to saying this affirmation silently in your mind and it will resonate within you—you will feel more connected. With this mantra, you are acknowledging who you are and accepting yourself in totality. Slowly you will truly start to believe it and find comfort in acceptance.

Lifelong: It is important to find beauty in the craziness of our lives. There's a lot to be said about embracing it all—yes, the hurriedness, the complications, the lousy moments, too, not only the happy, wondrous ones. It's a lifelong journey to find beauty in everything, but it is completely transformational once it becomes a part of your psyche. A way to practice this is by reflection. Stop right now and find something beautiful in this moment. Focus on it for a second. Then let it float away. The more you do this, the more you will train yourself to perceive the world with awe and bring more spirituality into your life. For example, this morning was really hectic. I was juggling the two kids, and my husband Joel, late to a very important meeting, needed me to move my car so he could get out of the driveway. So I had my infant and toddler on my body like monkeys, crying and covered head to toe in food from breakfast, while I was trying to get in my car. Joel was in a panic because he was late, and oh, he also lost his keys. . . . I bet you're feeling stress just from reading this. As I took a breath in the driver's seat of my car and watched him drive off, I looked down and realized my kids had stopped crying and were hugging each other across my body. They were actually giggling and smiling. The sun was streaming in my car. And my heart was filled with joy and gratitude. I just had to open my eyes to it. That was spiritual for me. Every night during the next week, before bed, jot down below the moments that really stood out to you each day and what was beautiful or miraculous about them. Challenge yourself to find grace in the mundane or even in the negative. It's all there right before your eyes; you just have to look for it. When it becomes part of your life, you become more connected, self-aware, secure, and resilient.

MONDAY _____

_____

TUESDAY _____

_____

WEDNESDAY _____

_____

THURSDAY _____

_____

FRIDAY _____

_____

SATURDAY _____

_____

SUNDAY _____

_____

Day 12

Flexibility

....

It's not the strongest of the species that survive, not the most intelligent but the one most responsive to change.

CHARLES DARWIN

A key component to resilience is to learn how to bend but not break. Flexibility gets to the core of being able to bound back from trauma—we have to be more like a rubber band. We always think about flexibility in physical ways such as yoga or touching your toes, but mentally, that's what resilient people are able to do—to adjust and adapt to have a successful outcome. What flexible thinking does is encourage us to change our behavior in response to a given situation that allows us to deal with the circumstances better. Studies have shown that resilient people are able to be flexible and change their emotional and physical reactions in response to the changing needs of various circumstances they are presented with.[1] In this way, flexibility buffers against stressful circumstances by helping regulate emotions and shifting our response to challenges.[2] Flexibility is a fundamental skill set in our ever-changing lives; otherwise we get stuck in a black-and-white version of our world, and this rigidity leads to poor resilience.

A woman once told me about her yearlong affair. She wasn't feeling loved by her husband of fifteen years; in fact, she felt neglected, devalued, even emotionally and verbally abused. Her husband was angry, rigid, shut down, and a workaholic. She tried talking about her feelings many times. He didn't listen; instead he was defensive and blamed her. She felt stuck. Their mutual friend Rob gave her a lot of attention. For years he had looked at her with a twinkle in his eye, but only recently, when he told her she didn't deserve to be treated with disrespect, did she dare to take it further. He valued her idiosyncrasies. He thought she was beautiful, smart, and talented. It wasn't even about the sex. She felt needed again. Wanted. Alive. Even her husband took notice and wondered what had changed. Needless to say, he found out about the affair after getting calls from other friends who had seen them together. She was reckless about where she went with her lover. It was almost as if she didn't care that her husband would eventually find out. Subconsciously she wanted him to.

He confronted her, and immediately she told him everything. It was in that exact moment when she saw the look in his eyes, she saw the man she had fallen in love with many years ago. He was fragile, vulnerable. He was broken, and she, too, from the pain she had caused. You can imagine the amount of work it took for them to become happy again, to learn to trust again, to love again, to respect and appreciate each other. They are still married today, and happy—because they ultimately learned to be flexible with each other. They were able to respond to the utmost pain and betrayal with some level of understanding, maturity, and open-mindedness. They had to learn to be flexible to change. When they had no choice but to finally confront their issues, they adapted to each other. They were resilient as individuals and as a couple. They were not only able to come back from the brink, but also were able to learn and grow from the experience. To become better people, to become a happier couple, and to thrive. Hopefully it doesn't always have to come to that point, but if it does, flexibility can drive endless possibilities for positive change.

It's hard to see in the trauma of the moment that life's challenges are always opportunities for growth. Abrupt changes open new doors, and resilient people are able to adapt to the varying tides and ride the waves of change. One of the most important lifelong skills we can learn is to accept change. Change is fixed. It's inevitable and constant. Whether it's gradual change that is barely noticeable, or dramatic and fast, it's happening all around us, and within us too. The key is to be aware of the changes and adapt to be more flexible.

Whenever you feel stuck, a flexible mind-set will help you readjust and inspire you to be creative about how you gain momentum again.

Take Stock

....

Are you flexible or rigid? Explain in what way below. A rigid person is stubborn. For example, if you're set on going to Paris for a vacation even though your husband makes a really good argument for going to San Francisco, you are pretty stubborn. A flexible person would evaluate the argument, be able to change his or her mind to embrace the better option in the given circumstances, and go to San Francisco.

_____

_____

_____

_____

_____

Do you embrace change or fear it? Avoid it? Describe:

_____

_____

_____

_____

What are some times in your life when you could have been more flexible?

_____

_____

_____

_____

_____

Would the outcome have been different, and if so, how?

_____

_____

_____

_____

_____

Daily Dos

Morning: Being flexible is fun—plus it spurs brain growth by encouraging new neural connections and exercising the ones you already have. One way to practice is by introducing more spontaneity. Try something new today. Learn a new language. Cook a new recipe. Try a new running route or a new machine at the gym. You can also try to change the order of your day, so if you usually work out at the end of the day, try morning. If you always have oatmeal for breakfast, try an egg on toast. You get the point.

What are you going to try new today?

Day: Give yourself a mental recess. Being flexible requires a break in attention to allow yourself to adapt to the changes at hand. Do something that allows you to take attention away from whatever is occupying your mind and relax for a moment. Look away from the computer. Go for a walk outside if you've been inside all day. Take a coffee or tea break. Do something that allows you to mentally shift. It will let your brain rest from what it's currently occupied with and be more refreshed when you return to the task at hand. This allows room for more creative, flexible thinking, and being more open to a change in perspective.

Night: Flexibility also has much to do with stepping out of your own shoes and seeing other people's viewpoints. What type of person are you? Do you usually dominate conversations? Do you hover over your children? Nag your spouse? Are you the type of friend who likes to call others, or do you expect friends to always call you? Note below five characteristics about yourself that you are willing to part with or improve.

1. _____

2. _____

3. _____

4. _____

5. _____

Lifelong: The sooner we accept change, the more flexible we become—and more resilient. It's comforting to know that pain isn't forever and that this, too, shall pass, as they say. Practice accepting change for what it is. Don't fight it. Welcome it, grow, and move forward. One exercise you can do daily is to evaluate what is changing for you that day. It can be something really simple and minor, or it can be major. Take a deep breath; observe what it is and your response. Practice acceptance, note any opportunity to learn from it, and then let go.

Perseverance

....

It's not that I'm so smart, it's just that
I stay with problems longer.

ALBERT EINSTEIN

There are endless great success stories of our time about those who have fought incredible odds to succeed. It's almost as if the hardships propelled them to thrive even more. J. K. Rowling wrote the first Harry Potter book in 1995, all the while going through a divorce, living in a small apartment with her son with the assistance of the government, and mourning her mom, who had recently passed away from multiple sclerosis. The manuscript was rejected by twelve different publishers. Not one, two, or even three. Twelve. (What would you have done at this point?) She succeeded in getting a publisher, but the advance was so small that they advised her to get a job to cover expenses. Nonetheless, she devoted most of her free time to writing the Harry Potter series. Instead of wallowing in her troubles, she weaved them into her books. She gave Potter her birthday—July 31—and he endured childhood traumas similar to hers. She pushed hard and never gave up. She was steadfast in her perseverance. Today, she is currently worth nearly $15 billion. She is the second-richest female entertainer on the planet, behind Oprah. I don't know J. K. Rowling so I can't comment on her personal life other than from speculation, but I hope that she is content and proud of how resilient she has been in the face of such odds. She had perseverance to ride out the uncertainty, and she was greatly rewarded for it (and, of course, some talent helps!).

It's easy to talk about how important it is to believe in yourself and what you're doing, and to never give up. The hard part is actually doing it. Getting pushed down many times and standing back up again and again is one of the hardest things to do in life. Why? Because failing confirms our deepest fears about ourselves—that we're inadequate, that we can't do it. It takes effort and energy to overcome this negative internal voice. The ones who do it well, and who are resilient, shine because of it. It's rare, if not impossible, to build strength and success without hard work.

Resilience relies on perseverance to move us forward. We can't bounce back from challenges unless we have momentum. Perseverance is that momentum. Although resilience and perseverance are distinct traits—not the same, as many might think—they do work closely together. Without momentum and steadfastness, without holding on to your course of action (perseverance), the ability to adapt to stress quickly and to be strengthened by our challenges (resilience) would not be able to occur effectively. A resilient person who lacks perseverance would be someone who is able to recover from trauma but who can't stay true to their initial vision and veers easily off course. Perseverance is the patience and dedication we require to optimize our fortitude.

What's a little counterintuitive, but equally as important, is that perseverance actually requires a bit of stubbornness, relentlessness, and rigidity—all qualities that you generally wouldn't think of when it comes to resilience. In some ways, rigidity helps us keep our eye on our goals and not deviate. But as you know from the previous chapter, it's also important to remain flexible—there should be a good balance. And as with the other attributes of resilience, perseverance is something we can work on and build. Read on to learn how.

Take Stock

Do you consider yourself a persistent person? What motivates you to keep going?

_____

_____

_____

_____

_____

Are you more likely to lose faith and stop trying when rejected, *or* do you try and try again until you achieve the outcome you want? Give a recent example.

_____

_____

_____

_____

_____

Have you created a list of meaningful goals? If not, let's do that now. Before you can develop persistence, you need to identify what you are willing to fight for. List your top three current goals that you can fulfill realistically this year. Make sure you're specific and that your goals are meaningful. For example, a goal of making a certain salary is not as practical as "getting a promotion within the year by consistently producing good work."

1. _____

_____

2. _____

_____

3. _____

_____

Daily Dos

Morning: Now that you know *what* you want, and you've thought about *why* you want to do it, it's time to move on to *how*. You need to develop an action plan. Take your list of goals and break it down into manageable tasks that you can achieve in less than an hour. And then take it a step farther and break those tasks into even smaller bits. Try doing a small task every day if you can. So sticking with the example of obtaining a promotion, you've already said that you want to do so by producing good work. Now advance that by explaining how you're going to measure the quality of your work. So this becomes "I would like to obtain a promotion within the next year by consistently producing good work, which will be measured by the fact that I feel proud of it and that my colleagues and boss provide positive feedback on it." This generates a positive outcome for the company, which will be x, y, or z (whether it be better client relationships, increased productivity, or however your business measures success). This is not a quick exercise, but once you do it, I promise that sticking to your goals will be so much easier! Let's execute this together now.

Goal 1

- What's the goal?

- Break it down into five tasks to help achieve that goal:

1A _____
1B_____
1C_____
1D_____
1E_____

- Now break each of these five tasks into two to five more bite-size chunks achievable in an hour or less.

1A can be achieved by doing:

a_____
b_____
c_____
d_____
e_____

1B can be achieved by doing:

a_____
b_____
c_____
d_____
e_____

1C can be achieved by doing:

a_____
b_____

c_____

d_____

e_____

1D can be achieved by doing:

a_____

b_____

c_____

d_____

e_____

1E can be achieved by doing:

a_____

b_____

c_____

d_____

e_____

- Go to your calendar and write down when you're going to tackle these smaller goals from the third section.

Now let's look at the *remaining goals*.

Goal 2

....

- Write down the goal here:

  _____

  _____

  _____

  _____

  _____

- Break it down into five tasks to help achieve that goal:

  2A _____

  2B _____

  2C _____

  2D _____

  2E _____

- Now break each of these five tasks into two to five more bite-size chunks achievable in an hour or less.

  2A can be achieved by doing:

  a_____

  b_____

  c_____

  d_____

  e_____

2B can be achieved by doing:

a_____
b_____
c_____
d_____
e_____

2C can be achieved by doing:

a_____
b_____
c_____
d_____
e_____

2D can be achieved by doing:

a_____
b_____
c_____
d_____
e_____

2E can be achieved by doing:

a_____
b_____
c_____

d_____

e_____

- Go to your calendar and write down when you're going to tackle these smaller goals from the third section.

Goal 3

- Write down the goal here:

_____

_____

_____

_____

_____

- Break it down into five tasks to help achieve that goal:

3A _____

3B _____

3C _____

3D _____

3E _____

- Now break each of these five tasks into two to five more bite-size chunks achievable in an hour or less.

3A can be achieved by doing:

a_____

b_____

c_____

d_____

e_____

3B can be achieved by doing:

a_____

b_____

c_____

d_____

e_____

3C can be achieved by doing:

a_____

b_____

c_____

d_____

e_____

3D can be achieved by doing:

a_____

b_____

c_____

d_____

e_____

3E can be achieved by doing:

a_____

b_____

c_____

d_____

e_____

- Go to your calendar and write down when you're going to tackle these smaller goals from the third section.

Day: Tell a few trusted, unbiased, positive friends or family about your top three goals that you're willing to share. While I don't always suggest sharing with others, when you're trying to build perseverance, having people to cheer you on and hold you accountable along the way is very helpful. This way you'll also be more motivated to press on. Talking through your goals will make them feel more achievable.

Night: Perseverance is a marathon, not a sprint, and requires a balance of mental strength, endurance, and discipline. It's easy to get sidetracked and lose focus. If you feel you have gone off course, evaluate why you did. Maybe you just needed to take a break, which is worthwhile, and it's really not going off course. Or maybe this isn't really a goal you deeply want after all. If it was just an act of dropping the ball, practice discipline. You can do so by making sure that you (1) follow through with whatever you seek to achieve. If you went off course, make sure it's for a good enough reason (it didn't fulfill my sense of purpose anymore; it started to take me away from my family life, etc.). (2) Reduce excuses. If you find yourself giving a lot of reasons why you didn't hold to your task, that is a sign of reduced lack of discipline. Cut the excuses and start talking yourself through all the reasons you started the task in the first place. This will help you stay on course. (3) Create a deadline if you don't have one already. This will help motivate you to persist and finish what you've set out to do.

Lifelong: Don't be so hard on yourself. It's a lifelong struggle to remind yourself that it's about the day to day, not the end goal. Once you achieve your goals, you'll create more. So make sure to avoid the trap of basing your happiness on the achievement. Once I lose ten pounds, I'll be happy. That never really works. Once we lose ten pounds, we'll want to lose three more. Our brain has become really good at shifting our goals and wanting more the minute we achieve what we want, so if we base our well-being just on achievements, we'll never be happy. Success is, of course, great—it's your reward for all your hard work—but remember to find contentment and meaning in the daily grind, in the struggle, in the sweat. Perseverance is a constant pursuit, but to truly be good at it, and to be resilient, requires that you enjoy the ride of your life, whatever your roller coaster may look like and however it may differ from what you envisioned.

Acceptance

....

Getting over a painful experience is much
like crossing monkey bars. You have to let go
at some point in order to move forward.

C. S. LEWIS

I had a client who had a really hard time in college because of her attention deficit hyperactivity disorder (ADHD). She didn't feel like she was capable of doing any better. She said she would sit at the library and study for hours, looking at the same material over and over again, but nothing was sinking in. She just doesn't have it in her, she said. It was painful to hear her say that. "I just can't." I felt like pulling out the children's classic *The Little Engine That Could,* and having her read and repeat over and over again, "I think I can, I think I can. . . . Yes you can!" She just didn't know how. She didn't know how to adjust her studying to complement her learning style. She felt hopeless. She was focusing on the grades, on the end result, on comparing how her friends were doing in class, instead of focusing on the learning process, on gaining knowledge that will enrich her life—on *her* learning process. She was focused on how to do things in the same way as people around her. She was defeated by her ADHD. She couldn't accept who she was and that she did things differently. She was not able to then use her reality to her advantage.

It's difficult to pinpoint why we have such a hard time with acceptance. It might be because guilt and shame, which we often feel to avoid acceptance, activate the part of our brain that deals with reward and reinforcement.[1] We have a chemical predisposition to become addicted to guilt and shame. Perhaps it's our culture of always wanting more, of wanting things to be different. Maybe we're uncomfortable with how unpredictable life really is, so we fight it instead. We deny or avoid most emotions because they don't make us *feel* good, wanting happiness so badly that we force it and in turn are just miserable. We're bombarded with surreal images to get us to believe in a dream, in a different version of how our lives should be. We're looking backward or forward instead of looking inward and enjoying our surroundings. Why is that? Perhaps we think that if we beat up on ourselves enough we'll actually change. But that's not how change happens. Change happens when we stop resisting and find the lessons waiting all around us.[2] Change happens when we choose to accept ourselves enough that we find peace—and are then able to see opportunities and open doors that we otherwise would miss because we're so caught up fighting ourselves.

This isn't about standing by idly. Acceptance isn't giving up. It's an active choice we make to release ourselves of a false sense of control, to stop fighting reality. We can still be accepting while also working diligently and effectively to bounce back, which is what resilient people do best. They balance acceptance with the qualities and skills I've discussed in these chapters. Resilience occurs when we accept that there are things we cannot change and that nothing is permanent. We are always moving forward. The choice is about *how* we choose to grow—to accept ourselves and our feelings, see the positive, and be proactive in our recovery, or to fight against growth, beat up on ourselves, blame our world, and be forlorn.

I recently saw the brilliant Pixar animated film called *Inside Out*. It's about a girl named Riley and her emotions—Joy, Sadness, Anger, Fear, and Disgust, who are actual characters who help Riley figure out her world. Throughout the movie, Joy tries to get Sadness to stay away from Riley, even drawing a circle for Sadness to stay contained within. Riley wants to run away from home after moving to a different city because of the Anger she feels, but ultimately what saves her from doing so is Sadness. Sadness prevents Riley from running away, brings her back to her family, and allows her to experience the deep sense of Joy that family connections and love can bring. At the end of the movie (sorry, spoiler), Joy accepts Sadness for who she is and understands that she's a very important part of Riley's experience. All the emotions ultimately accept one another in the movie, knowing they're a rich tapestry that makes Riley the well-balanced kid she is.

Acceptance makes moments of happiness turn into a lifetime of contentment that is richer. It's the difference between *feeling* happy and actually *being* happy. It's not about giving up but more about leaning into our current circumstances and feelings. Resilient people accept what *is;* they accept that nothing is permanent. Instead they focus on the lessons they can learn, how they can overcome, adapt, and move forward with grace.

Take Stock

Do you practice acceptance? What do you find the hardest to accept about yourself and your circumstances?

_____

_____

_____

_____

_____

Why is that so difficult for you to do?

_____

_____

_____

_____

_____

Do you believe that everything happens for a reason—or is that just a silly saying? Explain.

_____

_____

_____

_____

_____

List six characteristics about yourself that you accept and aren't trying to change—three strengths and three supposed weaknesses:

1. (strength) _____

2. (strength) _____

3. (strength) _____

4. (weakness) _____

5. (weakness) _____

6. (weakness) _____

Daily Dos

Morning: Don't focus so much on the *why*. While thinking about why things happen or why we are a certain way gives us great insight into ourselves and our world, focusing too much on it means we're living in yesterday, not today. We can't allow ourselves to get sucked into the reasons why something happened.

This moment is all we really have. Acceptance of what was and what is might be the only way to truly find contentment in our lives and to open ourselves to practice resilience in its fullest.

What two experiences in your life do you think most about in terms of why they happened?

1. _____

_____

_____

_____

_____

2. _____

_____

_____

_____

_____

Now that you've identified these two, can you make a conscious effort to accept them so they don't deplete any more of your energy? If it's hard for you to do, what's holding you back?

_____

_____

_____

_____

_____

Day: Acceptance has a lot to do with maintaining a positive outlook—while also seeing beauty in unusual things. When we're focused too much on what's lacking and what we need to fix, we don't appreciate all the good in our life. That makes it harder to practice acceptance and resilience. Let beauty in. Take a deep breath and just notice what's around you right now. Make note of what you see (this isn't a trick question):

_____

_____

_____

_____

_____

Now take on the eyes of a child—full of wonder and curiosity—and note what you see:

_____

_____

_____

_____

_____

Notice what things have changed even though you're still in the same place. It's really surprising to see the difference just with this one exercise. Try to practice this every day to see your world, and notice yourself, change before your very eyes.

Night: Acceptance isn't about sitting back and letting life go by. There's always something to learn from every experience, and finding those lessons is an important part of the resilience process. Let's say, for example, that you found out you were laid off at work, a job you've had long-term. It came as a surprise. How can you learn anything from this? How can acceptance help you here? Let's play it out. The emotions would start to flow . . . betrayal, anger, fear, insecurity, confusion, rejection, sadness. You naturally would question why. But none of your boss's answers or explanations would give you any ounce of comfort. The hardest thing to do in a time of pain is to accept—not to wish things weren't the way they are. The reality is that it deeply hurts. You can't change that. And it's important to accept that. This acceptance will help you focus on healing and shift your brain to find ways of recovering and learning. What you do have control over is how to move forward. In this way, acceptance will give you power. What can you learn? What can you apply to the process of finding another job, of finding a better fit for you? If you're having a hard time "learning" from the situation at hand, think about what you "notice." Sometimes just changing the word is helpful. Notice things about the situation and how you reacted. Simply *notice*. The things you notice are all valuable lessons, too.

Lifelong: Be kind to yourself. Choose not to judge what happens to you, your emotions, or your behavior. We're our own worst critics, expecting much of ourselves and being harsh when things don't pan out the way we expect them to. Instead of complaining—which is, really, a form of judgment—accept and remember that nothing is permanent. Resilient people don't resist what life throws at them. They're able to welcome their circumstances because they know that things are always in flux. They believe in themselves enough, and accept themselves enough, to know that they will ultimately persevere.

Week 3

SOCIAL

Innovation

....

Some men look at things the way they are and ask why.
I dream of things that are not and ask why not.

ROBERT F. KENNEDY

My husband loves watching the Discovery channel; one night
he started watching a documentary on birds. Since I'm not a
bird person, I was about to make a quick exit from the room,
but before doing so I caught the show's narrator describing a
study on how crows could get food in strange, difficult places.
I was intrigued. The narrator continued describing the experiment: First worms were placed in large, glass cylinders that
were then filled with water that didn't reach the very top.
When the crow tried to get his lunch, his beak was too short
to reach the worms floating at the top of the cylinder, and he
couldn't tip over the tube, since all the water would pour out,
and the worms then might be lost in the outpour. As part of the

experiment, pebbles were lying near the tubes. Unbelievably, the crow began dropping rock after rock in the tube until the water reached a height easy enough for him to finally snatch the worms floating on top. This totally blew my mind. The crows proved to be resourceful and innovative, which is at the heart of resilience.

Responding to new challenges requires innovation. If we were always faced with the same challenges, we'd already know how to overcome them easily. The types of challenges that stress us are the ones we've never been faced with before so we don't know how to handle them—and that's precisely why resilience requires creative thinking and innovative behavior.

Every great time period started with innovation: the Renaissance or the Gilded Age, for example. We have been able to evolve as a species, to be resilient as a civilization, mostly by being able to create and innovate. Arguably the most innovative person in this past century, Steve Jobs, used innovation to change the way the world operates on a global level. It's not just about being smart, as we well know. It's about seeing things in a new light, about remaining positive and pushing to change, to do better, to never give up. It's about resilience. Steve Jobs came back in when Apple was on its knees financially, and not only did he think about things in a different way, he also was able to focus that energy into rebounding from challenge—and all the while revolutionizing how we interact with the world.

How can we learn from Jobs? Instead of letting stress overtake us, start looking at things differently. Innovation catapults us out of the challenging situation and helps us move forward.

Innovation is progress no matter what the circumstances, and often in the worst of times. It is resilience at its best.

Aside from helping us solve problems effectively, innovation can also be a wonderful outlet for emotional distress. We've all known and hear of brilliant writers, artists, and composers such as Ernest Hemingway, Edgar Degas, and Sergey Rachmaninoff creating masterpieces in the darkest of times while suffering from depression. They were creators—but their creations were also innovative because they influenced change and started something new: Hemingway paved the way for the modern relaxed style in twentieth-century fiction, and Degas is credited as one of the founders of Impressionism. Their innovations gave them an escape from their pain. Had they just kept their creative thoughts in their heads, and not followed through with their art, they probably wouldn't have been able to be as resilient in the time of struggle. Stifling their creativity, they wouldn't have had an outlet in which to channel their pain. They certainly wouldn't have left a legacy that enriches and inspires so many generations.

Take Stock

How creative are you? Trick question. We're all creative, as children. And then a majority of us do unfortunately stop being as creative because we get bogged down by other things. Our minds also get less creative when we don't exercise our imagination. The good news is that all of us can be more creative and ultimately innovative; we just have to work at it, like anything else. There are some ways to see where you're at on the scale of creativity other than whether or not you like to create things:

Do you have an issue with someone telling you what to do?
NEVER/OCCASIONALLY/FREQUENTLY/ALWAYS

Do you find beauty in ordinary things?
NEVER/OCCASIONALLY/FREQUENTLY/ALWAYS

Do you enjoy watching people and listening to conversations?
NEVER/OCCASIONALLY/FREQUENTLY/ALWAYS

Are you easily inspired by the world around you?
NEVER/OCCASIONALLY/FREQUENTLY/ALWAYS

Do you like to break stereotypes and make your own rules?
NEVER/OCCASIONALLY/FREQUENTLY/ALWAYS

Are you expressive?
NEVER/OCCASIONALLY/FREQUENTLY/ALWAYS

Do you take time to just think (and not do anything else)?
NEVER/OCCASIONALLY/FREQUENTLY/ALWAYS

Do like enjoy challenging others?
NEVER/OCCASIONALLY/FREQUENTLY/ALWAYS

Are you someone who likes to try new things?
NEVER/OCCASIONALLY/FREQUENTLY/ALWAYS

Have your creations been tested? Do others reap the benefits of what you created?

NEVER/OCCASIONALLY/FREQUENTLY/ALWAYS

Are you able to take your creative works and share them with others?

NEVER/OCCASIONALLY/FREQUENTLY/ALWAYS

Are other people receptive to your creations?

NEVER/OCCASIONALLY/FREQUENTLY/ALWAYS

If you're closer to the "always" side of your answers, then you're most likely on the higher end of the creativity spectrum. Your challenge is then how to hone your creative abilities. For those of you on the lower end of the spectrum, work on reigniting your creativity by practicing my prescriptions below.

Daily Dos

Morning: To be more creative, you must expose yourself to different ideas. Do you always read the same types of books or blogs? The same magazines? Watch the same shows? If so, make an effort to broaden your horizons. By making changes to what you read and watch, you're stimulating your mind to look at things differently, which spurs creativity and innovation. For example, if you usually take notes during work meetings in a conference room, try something different for a change of pace. If you are able to, take your next meeting outside—without your computer. Maybe you'll notice your ideas will flow better, or you'll have a particularly interesting brainstorming session because you're not looking at your computer and taking notes. Record the meeting on your smartphone to keep track of ideas you can make note of at a later time. You'll be surprised how you can find inspiration in the most unassuming places. The best ideas sometimes come from these unexpected places. How many times have you heard a fashion designer talk about getting inspiration for her prints from her travels, or an architect being motivated by natural forms from a hike? Changing things will shift your perspective, open your mind, and allow creativity to flourish. Write down what you're going to do today that's different from what you typically do.

_____

_____

_____

_____

_____

Day: Often we censor ourselves before we can even develop a good idea or an innovative way to solve a problem. Next time you're in a rut and feel yourself using negative words such as "no," "but," "sorry," "done," or "end," try the "yes, and" technique. Improv classes teach this all the time—and I love it for improving my creativity. Start with an idea or a problem, something like "I am feeling lonely in my life." Continue with something starting in "yes, and," such as "Yes, and that makes me feel sad, especially at night." Challenge yourself to continue using "yes, and" statements. "Yes, and I hope that I can feel less sad about it in the future," "Yes, and maybe I can start making more friends at work." Let your imagination run wild. This will help you build on your thoughts and feelings, and even envision usually bland or negative situations in a more positive, action-oriented way.

Night: Do something you used to enjoy as a child. Take up painting again, or the piano. It should be something that allows you to get creative, relax, and really get immersed in that activity. Write down that activity, and plan what day you're going to pick it up again. Don't procrastinate. Not only will it help open your heart and mind to innovation and resilience, but it will also improve your health and happiness levels.

Lifelong: The best thing you can do over time is to relax your mind. Don't try so hard. Some of the greatest innovations in history, including the sewing machine, the lightbulb, and even more recent innovations in technology, were all products of their inventor's dreams, even Google! The April 9, 2012, edition of *Fortune* magazine published a story on how Larry Page and Sergey Brin got the idea for "downloading the entire web onto computers." Larry Page dreamed it one night when he was twenty-three years old. Don't get me wrong—innovation also comes with great focus, discipline, and patience. But don't be so hard on yourself. Take a deep breath, get a good night's sleep—and have a pen and paper by your bedside table just in case you need to write down last night's amazing dream. It might just give you the answer to a crisis or show you a different way to solve a problem.

Emotional Intelligence

....

*Somehow our society has formed a one-sided view of
the human personality, and for some reason everyone
understood giftedness and talent only as it applied to the
intellect. But it is possible not only to be talented in one's
thoughts but also to be talented in one's feelings as well.*

LEV VYGOTSKY

The other day I was shopping at our local mall, picking up
something for a friend's birthday. As I was perusing the racks,
a group of teenage boys passed by, and I caught a snippet of
their conversation. "She was so lame, she said she didn't want
to be my girlfriend." Friend replies, "Dude, weren't you pissed?
Is she with another guy?" Answer: "Whatever. I don't care.
Yeah, I was mad. I'll get over it." Trust me, I've heard adults
talk like this too. It made me think about the type of vague,

nondescript language we use to talk about our emotions and feelings. Not just to one another, but most importantly, to ourselves. The words we use build the framework from which we function and see the world. This emotional vocabulary is an integral part of emotional intelligence.

Emotional intelligence (EI) is a critical skill of resilient people. It involves a multilevel process—the ability to be able to monitor the feelings of yourself and others, to discriminate among them, and to use that information when you act. Though the level of emotional intelligence varies from person to person, we all use it when coping with negative circumstances. Researchers have shown that highly resilient people tend to utilize more emotionally intelligent behaviors in times of stress. They are able to use their emotional intelligence more acutely, and in a targeted fashion, to learn from life's setbacks and cope more effectively. Resilient people understand the benefits associated with positive emotions and use this awareness to their advantage when coping with negative emotional events.[1] For example, fights between spouses are a natural part of marriage. For some couples, fights can strengthen the relationship. For others, they can be the demise of it. For those who learn and build from their disagreements, often it is because they are using emotional intelligence to their advantage, as well as using a positive framework. They are able to clearly communicate their emotions and get to the root of the issue, and they are empathetic and attuned enough to their spouse to understand their perspective. They understand that it's the heat of the moment, that they love their spouse, and that they'll work together to get through it. Through the anger, pain, hurt, or whatever else they feel, they remain optimistic.

Translating feelings into even just one or two words literally calms the part of our brain that controls emotions, which greatly reduces their influence over us.[2] There are more than one hundred words for different emotions—and all have subtle distinctions. Being able to differentiate among these various emotions—to be able to understand the difference between feeling excited and feeling proud, or conversely, being able to distinguish between feeling angry and feeling frustrated—is called emotional granularity. It's not just about knowing words but also being able to differentiate among their subtle differences, such as the distinction involved in being irritable, upset, or anxious. A person with low emotional granularity would just describe these feelings with a generic word such as "good" or "mad." These minor differences matter. Studies show that when we learn to distinguish among specific emotions both within ourselves and in others, we are less likely to react without thinking and are more likely to think through our options before acting on our emotions or the situation.[3] Being able to respond deliberately and thoughtfully—rather than just responding immediately—has been associated with making more effective decisions, and ultimately increases our resilience.

Take Stock

Let's figure out your EI. Below is a list of behaviors exhibited by highly emotionally intelligent people. Don't worry if you don't practice all of these behaviors, or even any of them. That's why you're reading this book! Think about your behavior over the course of a year as you answer each question.

You're curious about people.   YES NO

You know how to differentiate between
thoughts and feelings.   YES NO

You're not afraid of negative emotions or
feelings. (See below in the "Morning" section
for a more detailed description.)   YES NO

You have empathy.   YES NO

You can tell easily when loved ones are upset.   YES NO

You don't react immediately to situations.   YES NO

You're a good leader.   YES NO

You know your weaknesses.   YES NO

You are not easily distracted.   YES NO

When you get mad or upset, you know
what caused it.   YES NO

You know your values, and you are a
moral person.   YES NO

You handle conflict well.   YES NO

You're good at reading facial expressions.   YES NO

You don't let your negative feelings take
over your entire mind-set.   YES NO

You trust your gut—and others do, too.   YES NO

These are some of the elements that go into having a high
EI. If you answered "no" to more questions than "yes," you need
to make a concerted effort to build your EI.

Daily Dos

Morning: When you have an intense feeling—good or bad—
ask yourself, "What am I really feeling?" Try to get very specific, down to even the physical sensations you're experiencing,
and differentiate among microemotions. The more you practice this, the easier it will become. Remember those sentence
diagrams you drew in grade school? Think of them as you try
to be more descriptive—one word at the top, branching down
into more descriptive words, including physical sensations
and the most detailed you can be about your feelings. Be careful not to confuse thoughts with feelings. Feelings are what
gives you an emotional response; thoughts are your cognitive
response. For example, how do you feel about your divorce?
Your initial response might be that you feel like your life is
turned upside down and that you won't be able to recover. But
those are actually your thoughts. What you're feeling are the
emotions behind those thoughts, feelings such as anger, disap-
pointment, pain, or rejection.

Start now by writing down what you are feeling. The more detailed, the better.

_____

_____

_____

_____

_____

Day: Now that you have done your morning exercise to practice getting specific about what you're feeling in the moment, take that one step farther and learn to differentiate among negative emotions specifically. Often people think that their negative feelings are generally angry or sad, but there are so many other feelings within that spectrum, such as abandonment, envy, cynicism, or bafflement. Next time you're experiencing a negative emotion, try to narrow down what you're actually feeling, and don't shy away from those negative feelings. Acceptance gives us understanding. Understanding is power—when we take power away from those negative feelings, when we don't let them take over our lives, it makes it easier for us to move on from them. The key to resilience is accepting the negative, learning from it, and then using that knowledge to move forward without rejecting or ignoring the pain. Fill in the blanks for your own negative situation now:

- Initial feeling _____
- Specific emotion after consideration _____

- Notes on understanding/accepting the feeling _____

_____

Night: Build up your emotional vocabulary. Try to remember a new word that describes an emotion every day. There are many resources online to help with this. After dinner but an hour or two before bedtime so you're not too tired—say, at 9:00 P.M.—set a stopwatch for three minutes and really feel whatever emotion you're experiencing at the moment. Write down everything you notice in those three minutes. Be very specific. You might start out thinking you're sad, but after being more thoughtful, you might realize that you're actually only tired. Being able to improve your emotional granularity is a powerful skill set.

Lifelong: Take the time right now to remember an experience in which you felt very strong emotions. Work through the story of the event in your mind, writing down all of the various feelings you may have had. For example, say your boss told you to rewrite a proposal you thought you aced. You felt upset. Now challenge yourself to dig deeper. Did you actually feel disappointed? Rejected? Hurt? Devalued? Get as detailed as possible. This exercise will, over time, help you be more emotionally aware, encourage better communication with others, and help you bounce back from challenges much quicker with strength and focus. These are critical skills that build resilience long-term.

Purpose

....

Ever more people today have the means to live,
but no meaning to live for.

VIKTOR E. FRANKL

My selfless cousin had purpose. His primary purpose was to give to others. He tragically drowned in a swimming accident on his fortieth birthday, leaving five young children and his wife. His death was shattering, but in its wake we got a rare glimpse into what an extraordinary man he was. Only after his death did we find out that he had started an anonymous charity fund that not even his wife knew about. He would distribute money monthly to destitute families through someone who would assist him in getting the funds to them so they wouldn't know who the donor was. He was not a wealthy man by any means. But he always had enough to help others and create memorable experiences. He thought of even the simplest yet powerful deeds. Everyone in his neighborhood knew a certain store gave out free helium balloons to each child on his or her birthday. Many of the children in his area came from low-income families, so the balloons were a source of much joy and merriment to all. We found out that at the end of each month, he would go to the store and secretly pay for that month's balloons. These altruistic stories go on and on, from secret tuition payments, to undercover sponsored marriage counseling sessions, to covertly paying for a family's admission to an amusement park because they couldn't afford it. Such discreet but impactful, consistent charity is a rarity; he is a shining example of living with purpose.

Purpose gives our lives value. It provides a clear and targeted direction. It keeps our attention focused on forward thinking versus inward or backward thinking. To have a higher purpose, whether it be spiritual or not, helps a person maintain course. Even when plans get sidetracked, purpose helps to refocus and continue on. That's at the heart of resilience.

In the face of great tragedy, purpose can prove powerfully helpful in recovery. Candace Lightner founded Mothers Against Drunk Driving (MADD) as a response to her thirteen-year-old daughter being killed by a drunk driver. She vowed to bring awareness to this major issue, and she did. In the face of such unthinkable pain, she was able to move forward by finding her new purpose and acting on it. MADD says that drunk driving has been cut in half since the organization's founding. Not only did purpose help Lightner endure, but it also saved countless lives.

Purpose not only improves the ability to bounce back, but it also keeps us healthy: a recent study was done looking at how having a purpose in life influences our health, specifically susceptibility to having a stroke. This robust study used data from almost seven thousand people over age fifty who were stroke-free at the time the data was collected. Results show that the higher a person's sense of purpose, the less likely the person was going to have a stroke.[1] Another study showed that having a greater sense of purpose is linked to a reduced risk of mild cognitive impairment and Alzheimer's disease.[2] Even when researchers have studied something as complex as pain tolerance, it was having purpose in life that stood out in increasing healthy individuals' pain tolerance.[3]

In today's complicated world, finding purpose can be very difficult. Everything has changed. Our relationships mostly exist via web. Some argue they lack meaning. How many more times have you "liked" or commented on a friend's post rather than picked up the phone to call her or gone so far as to meet her in person? We have replaced human connection with screens—and it's that very human connectivity that adds to purpose in life. Since technology is inevitable, it's important we don't just get caught up in comparing ourselves and holding relationships at a distance. Use technology as a resource to foster better connections, as a tool to help others, by getting involved in benevolent campaigns or making supportive comments on others' pictures. Or perhaps seeing someone else's plight will encourage you to find purpose and meaning you otherwise wouldn't have been aware of.

Purpose is something we connect to beyond ourselves—be it about being a mom, a good employee, or something outside our daily world, such as the environment or animals. But there is a crucial extra step to take to have purpose: feeling upset about the water drought in California, for example, is one thing, but making a choice to conserve water, mobilize the community, and do more, is another. Living with purpose means your behavior helps attain your goals. Your ideals steer your actions. That's living with purpose, and it is integral to living with resilience.

Take Stock

Do you have a strong sense of purpose? Take the quiz below to see.

Do you feel like your life has meaning?

NEVER/OCCASIONALLY/FREQUENTLY/ALWAYS

Do you volunteer, or are you involved in charity?

NEVER/OCCASIONALLY/FREQUENTLY/ALWAYS

Do you pray or meditate?

NEVER/OCCASIONALLY/FREQUENTLY/ALWAYS

Do you like your job?

NEVER/OCCASIONALLY/FREQUENTLY/ALWAYS

Do you think your work is important and meaningful?
NEVER/OCCASIONALLY/FREQUENTLY/ALWAYS

Do you enjoy intimate, long-term relationships that add
value to your life?
NEVER/OCCASIONALLY/FREQUENTLY/ALWAYS

Are you close to your family?
NEVER/OCCASIONALLY/FREQUENTLY/ALWAYS

Do you see beauty in your world?
NEVER/OCCASIONALLY/FREQUENTLY/ALWAYS

Do you often do what makes you happy, what makes you
smile?
NEVER/OCCASIONALLY/FREQUENTLY/ALWAYS

Are you inspired by something or someone?
NEVER/OCCASIONALLY/FREQUENTLY/ALWAYS

Are you committed to a particular cause or person? Do
you fulfill your commitments?
NEVER/OCCASIONALLY/FREQUENTLY/ALWAYS

Do you feel like you make the world a better place?
NEVER/OCCASIONALLY/FREQUENTLY/ALWAYS

If most of your answers fell on the right side of the spectrum,
your life is rich with focus, purpose, and value. If not, don't
fear. Let's brush up on ways we can all add purpose to our lives.

Daily Dos

....

Morning: Take a moment in bed or in the shower to think about something you value. Just one thing. Is it family time? Singing? Or gardening? Being affectionate with your spouse? Focus your thought on that. It only takes a few minutes. Subconsciously work is being done, and it will infuse your day with some level of direction and purpose. As you repeat this day to day, what you value most will remain on the top of your mind without your even needing to think about it.

Day: Passion helps you find purpose. What are you passionate about in your life? Do it as often as you can within reason. If you're passionate about exploring the world, plan a trip once a year at a minimum. Write down your dates and other details. If you're passionate about the environment, what can you do to help? Make a plan. If you have a hard time finding what your passions are, like so many of us, try answering simple questions that give you clues, such as: If you could read a book about anything, what would it be about? When you were a kid, what did you enjoy playing with or doing?

Night: Research has found spirituality is related to purpose. Do a spiritual meditation. But if you're not religious, don't worry. Connectivity to something beyond yourself is the key element of spirituality—it infuses our life with meaning. If it's not God or your version of God or a higher power, it can be the Earth or nature, family, integrity, honesty. Before bed, connect with something beyond yourself, and focus on that concept for a minute or two. If you believe in God, say a prayer. If you're not sure about God, focus on an event or activity that really moved you during the day, something you felt was a spiritual experience. If you have a hard time with spirituality, just focus on something that brings you peace, such as the last time you were sitting and watching the ocean. Let it infuse your mind and heart. This will help encourage a sense of purpose and meaning—and also lead to better sleep!

Lifelong: Finding purpose is not an easy pursuit. It's even harder to actually live it. Building off of your "Day" exercise, now create a mission statement of purpose for your life. And try to live it every day. To do this and home in on what really matters to you, answer these questions honestly:

What do you love to do? _____

If you had to give yourself a reason to live, what would it be? _____

What would you stand for? _____

What principles do you hold highest? _____

What brought you immense joy as a kid? _____

What were you doing when you lost track of time? _____
_____

If you had all the money in the world, how would you spend your time? _____

What would your perfect day look like? Describe every detail. _____

What makes you feel sadness if you are without? _____

_____

Once you have made notes about what gives you meaning, create a mission statement. This is my mission statement: "My purpose is to live a life rich with meaning; to maintain a healthy family unit by being an engaged mother and wife and to help others strengthen resilience and well-being. I will do so with grace, humility, compassion, love, courage, and integrity."

What's yours?

_____
_____
_____
_____
_____

Problem Solving

....

The problem is not that there are problems.
The problem is expecting otherwise and thinking
that having problems is a problem.

THEODORE RUBIN

When adversity strikes, we all have different ways of handling it. But some of us are better at dealing with it than others. What's the differentiating factor? Good problem-solving skills. Research shows that people who are able to come up with solutions are better able to cope than those who simply go through the motions or wait for a problem to resolve itself. To problem solve (as it applies to resilience) means to *actively* try to find a solution to a challenge. Resilient people are able to figure out creative solutions to a problem that will lead to a positive outcome. In this way they are able to reduce uncertainty and vulnerability to further risk.[1]

People who are resilient and have a good ability to cope are better at tackling daily stress. In the research, problem solving is treated as a skill or coping resource, just as good communication is.[2] If you are good at problem solving, you have good coping resources; you are able to resolve issues well. Making decisions is physically calming according to neurological research, and it makes us more effective problem solvers. Additionally, being decisive helps us combat activity in a region of our brain that has a tendency to pull us toward negative behaviors, and anything done to counteract that is beneficial.[3] It's important to note that having good problem-solving skills doesn't always mean you're able to take action and use them in a crisis. People often get paralyzed by turmoil. What resilient people are able to do especially well is actually make good use of the skills they already possess, such as good problem solving, and do so in a focused, quick way that helps them overcome whatever adversity they are faced with at the moment.

To understand resilience, we need to understand what happens to us when a crisis occurs. When challenges hit, our fight-or-flight response gets triggered. It's a human, natural response to pain and fear. The response is triggered by the release of hormones that prepare you to either stay and deal with a threat or to run away to safety. The stress is actually a helpful response, making you better equipped to deal with the situation at hand. The influx of hormones heightens your sensitivity to the world around you so you can respond quickly to the crisis—or shut down. What resilient people are able to do differently is control this biological response. Where others panic and clamp up, resilient people stay calm. Resilience helps maximize our innate fight-or-flight response—to be acutely aware of details, quickly understand what's happening, and come up with solutions.

Even in nonthreatening situations, it's critical to be flexible with your problem solving so you are able to take advantage of opportunities that come up that might shift your strategy. Favorable circumstances could present themselves that you might have otherwise missed, which could lead to even better opportunities than you had imagined. But you need to stay open to them. For example, when I was in graduate school I had always imagined having an academic career in which I would solely do research and have a clinical practice. Midway through my studies, I unexpectedly met someone who soon became my mentor and introduced me to the media world, through which I could share my expertise with a broader audience and hopefully affect many lives. Had I not been open to this, I would not have the career that I love today.

Take Stock

A good rule of thumb for building problem-solving skills is to write down a list of possible solutions when faced with a challenge. Keep it short and concise so your brain can process it more easily. Always include one resolution that seems out of the box for you—it might just be the one that ends up working best. If you're really stuck, ask a friend who generally makes good decisions—he or she can be valuable in helping you see things in a different way. Envision the outcome you want, and work backward to find scenarios that can help you get there. Add pros and cons to each. Doing this regularly will help you greatly in strengthening your problem-solving skills; the process of writing and visualizing will help organize solutions and thoughts to support resilience.

Let's see how your problem-solving skills rate.

Describe in detail a current challenge or crisis you are faced with:

_____

_____

_____

_____

_____

What is the outcome you want?

_____

_____

_____

_____

_____

Now write down four possible solutions to get you to this outcome. Remember to be concise but detailed with your solutions and include one that is out of the box:

1. _____

_____

_____

_____

_____

2. _____

_____

_____

_____

_____

3. _____

_____

_____

_____

_____

4. Out-of-the-box option: _____

_____

_____

_____

_____

Was that hard for you? Easy? You'll be able to tell from this exercise how much you need to work on this skill. We all could use some practice. Focus on your progress every step of the way while planning your next steps, rather than becoming weighed down by the amount of work that is required.

Daily Dos

Morning: To help yourself have the courage to tackle an immediate issue, reverse negative thinking by adding an empowering "and I will" to the end of the problem statement. Let's say you are having trouble finishing a report for work. Instead of just saying, "This is so tough," add to it an empowerment statement: "This is so tough, and I will find the strength to handle it." Improvisation classes do this type of exercise a lot because it's helpful to create a story line. In life, it's very helpful, too. It'll help shift your attention to a positive, actionable resolution for the crisis at hand and will help you find creative solutions that you wouldn't previously have thought of.

Day: To reduce distractions when problem solving in a busy place (ahem, new open office plans sprouting up everywhere!), put blinders on to help you focus: close your eyes, frame them with open palms, or put earphones on and listen to white noise. Focus on what is specifically challenging. If it's nothing specific, focus your attention on something calming, such as the sky outside your window, to rid yourself of distractions. Train your mind to quiet down in a chaotic moment or time of stress. It'll help you maintain calm and focus and be better able to tackle problems.

Night: When facing a challenge that doesn't need an immediate response, take the time to think about it. We're often pressured to find answers in the stress of a moment, even if one isn't needed right away. The pressure comes from our natural fight-or-flight response and also from the burden we put on ourselves to make quick decisions. Speed doesn't always equal quality. Give yourself time to sleep on something. You need time to process different scenarios in your mind, and that can't always be done quickly. Plus, new ideas can actually come to you while you sleep. (People are often most creative late at night and can dream of good solutions.)

Lifelong: We are our own best coach. Silently coach yourself through the challenge in the moment, as strange as it might feel—phrases such as "Stay with it," "You can do this," "You've done harder things in life," "You are worth it," or "Your family loves you" can prove extremely helpful in rallying resilience. I'll never forget the death crawl scene from *Facing the Giants* when the coach blindfolds the football player and helps him carry another player on his back while crawling across the field. The player thought he was only going to a portion of it. He had a preconceived expectation about how far he was able to go, which wasn't very far at all, so when he approached that length without being blindfolded, he started to give up. But when he was blindfolded and was not able to see or measure his performance, his coach was able to talk him through it, asking him just to do his very best and keep going until he couldn't anymore. And sure enough, he went the entire length of the field, much to his complete shock. He didn't even know what he was capable of. When he was able to see, he had let himself get in the way of truly achieving his best.

Social Connectivity

I want to be around people that do things.
I don't want to be around people anymore that judge
or talk about what people do. I want to be around people
that dream and support and do things.

AMY POEHLER

I'm fiercely independent, and my loved ones know that I'm not good at asking for help. In fact, I'm so bad at it that my closest friends don't even ask if I need help anymore—they just show up. Social support is critical to resilience, because having caring, supportive people around us is protective during a crisis. While our friends may not be able to actually change anything, their simply listening to the situation and providing supportive words or positive feedback is an important part of being able to bounce back from adversity.

Social support even affects our neurobiology. Many studies have shown across the board that social support is a crucial ingredient to mental and physical health in the time of any kind of crisis or risk.[1] Social support biologically and hormonally changes us, making us stronger to endure the negative symptoms that come from stress and trauma. How does it do this? We release a multitude of hormones when we feel love and are understood by another. These hormones make us feel happier. They not only change our internal ecosystem, but also bond us together with others. By sharing and expressing love and support, we are strengthening our connections, and in turn reinforcing our personal self-esteem and identity. By feeling connected, we feel stronger and are better able to rebound from trauma. This is how deep, thoughtful, reliable relationships boost our resilience.

It's not about quantity or being able to brag about how many friends you had at your last birthday party. Rather, how many of those friends would pull through for you when you really need them? Think of your social support as a spider-web. Your deepest relationships form the strongest connections in that web that supports you. People who have a lot of friends but lack deep relationships might have a lot of strands but feel insecure subconsciously because they know that at any moment, the floor beneath them, their web of support, can break. If we have few but strong strands (i.e., relationships), we might not have a lot of room to spread out, but we definitely feel secure, and we know how to tread carefully on that web so it provides the steady support we need to thrive. It is those people with strong webs, not necessarily the ones with the most strands, who are most resilient. And when it comes to social support, research has shown that with marriage, interestingly enough, the most protective relationship for a man is with his spouse. For a woman, it's with a close female friend, regardless of whether she's married or not.[2] Women tend to share more and feel more empathy and compassion with their friends, more so than even with their spouse.

It's important to take stock of who really matters in your life, and then nurture those relationships throughout your life. Constant communication isn't always best either. Some of my closest friends or family and I don't connect for weeks, even months, but when we do—it's as if we never stopped and we're right back to the same level of connectivity. There's no guilt involved, no hard feelings. Keeping up with our dearest relationships provides a necessary and strong foundation from which we can be resilient and deal with challenges. Without the support, help, reassurance, or just listening ear of others, we can only do so much. It takes a village, it really does. Just make sure your village is an authentic and positive one.

Take Stock

Let's assess the depth and status of your social network. No, I'm not talking about social media followers! That has very little to do with resilience, actually. Popularity gives people a false sense of being appreciated, so it provides a little (and short-lived) self-esteem boost—but it doesn't provide the power and confidence that solid, authentic social support gives. So let's forget your "followers" for a moment and think about your real relationships.

1. Make a list in the box below of your closest confidants, the ones you can rely on in a crisis, through thick and thin. They can be family or friends.*

2. Now evaluate the list—do you have a strong support group or not?

   a. If you do not, think about what has prevented you from sustaining lasting, deep relationships.

   b. Reach out to reconnect with people in your past who were good friends but with whom you have since lost touch because of external circumstances.

---

* Don't pay any attention to how many you have (that's precisely why I haven't made a numbered list for you—the number doesn't matter!). It could be two. It could be five. But rarely is it more than ten if we're really being honest with ourselves.

c. Join a class so you can meet like-minded people who are interested in similar things as you.

d. If you are more of an introvert, challenge yourself to start small talk with someone at work or at your religious institution whom you find interesting.

Daily Dos

Morning: Today, vow to ask for help and be of help. Asking for assistance is particularly hard to do for many people. It can be something simple like "I ran out of milk; can you please drop off a gallon today?" to something more serious, such as "I'm having trouble in my marriage. I need to talk to someone, but I don't want you to say anything back to me, I don't want to hear your opinions. I just need you to listen to me." Think about what you need this morning, and actually act on it. Do you need someone to just listen and not speak, or advice on how to move forward? Positive feedback or constructive criticism? Reach out now. Resilient people are fiercely independent. But one of their biggest strengths is also knowing when, who, and how to ask for help when needed. Additionally, it's important to be of help and have a healthy amount of give and take. Randomly reach out to three people you cherish, and ask how you can be helpful to them this week. Even if they refuse the help (try to insist on doing at least something, even if it's small), it strengthens connectivity and thus resilience. Let them know they can rely on you. And in turn you have strengthened your bond and know you can rely on them.

Day: We do physical health checks. Why not check into the health of our relationships? Our exchanges with people in our lives ebb and flow naturally. We're not always going to stay in close touch, and that's entirely normal, especially when things get particularly busy. Some of our best friends aren't necessarily ones with whom we communicate constantly. It's not about how often you stay in touch. It's about the quality of your connectivity. The fundamentals of a healthy relationship include taking responsibility for your emotions and behaviors, being empathetic, supportive, kind, and giving. Do you have fun together? Is there trust? Do you feel appreciated and understood? If you're in a relationship, whether it be friendship or romantic, that feels exhausting or fills you with guilt, or one in which you're often upset, disappointed, or hurt, it's important to reevaluate what's keeping you engaged with that person. Is it that you've been friends since high school and you feel an obligation even though the relationship has become tiresome? There can be a variety of reasons. The important thing is to learn to recognize when it is over or, worse, has become toxic. It can be very hard ending relationships, especially when there are deep feelings involved. Sometimes it's easier to let things die down if you're comfortable with that; other times it requires verbal closure face to face. Whatever needs to happen, it's important to do it sooner rather than later. Resilient people fill their lives with positive relationships that are enriching and supportive.

Night: Turn off all electronics and connect with your spouse or partner tonight by recalling a special memory. If you don't have a spouse or partner, invite over a good friend or relative, someone who means a lot to you. Share a funny story or a touching moment, or look through some old photos together. This is one of the best ways to reconnect and nurture cherished relationships.

Lifelong: Working off your list in the "Take Stock" section, jot down when you last connected with those people. Was it through the phone? Text? E-mail? Facebook? Now select a time frame during which you're going to reach out again—and list how you're going to do that. Be proactive about keeping in touch and finding ways to see each other. Write in your calendar "date nights" with the people in your life who really matter. Try to see each person at least once every month or two. Also, think about a deep, authentic friendship that you don't have in your life anymore. What changed? Is it worth reconnecting? Will that relationship enrich your life? If you think it will, pick up the phone and say hello. That's always the hardest thing to do, especially when a long time has gone by, but odds are that person misses you, too.

Day 20

Altruism

....

The best way to find yourself is to lose yourself
in the service of others.

MAHATMA GANDHI

Altruism is driven by empathy. Empathy involves our ability to notice and correctly interpret the needs and desires of other people as if you were stepping into their shoes and trying to understand what they are going through. For instance, an empathetic person may see a homeless man and know he is hungry and needs human connectivity. Altruism takes this knowledge further and acts upon it, by offering the homeless man acknowledgment and something to eat. Altruism is the *practice* of concern rather than just the feeling of being concerned. Altruistic people give freely of their time, energy, or money, without any expectation of return. It's doing for the sake of doing, not for any direct, premeditated benefit of your own.

Altruism and empathy amplify our overall happiness and contribute greatly to our ability to maintain resilience over time. How? First, by focusing on others, we are focusing less on ourselves and thus getting some "breathing room" away from our own challenges, whatever they may be. This allows us to regroup and reboot, and perhaps even find some fresh perspective on those challenges. Because of that needed time, it also counteracts the negative effects that stress can have on us.

Giving to others has powerful benefits on your mental and physical health. It also increases your sense of purpose, which, we know from a previous chapter, improves resilience as well. Studies have shown that giving was actually more strongly linked to mental health than receiving therapy.[1] But obviously, make sure to give what you're able without depleting yourself. If you don't have money to donate, try donating your time instead. If you don't have time to donate right now, think about other ways you can help.

If empathy and altruism are part of building resilience, is it really something we can work on, or is it something we are just born with? Researchers at the Max Planck Institute for Evolutionary Anthropology in Germany tested this idea. They did an experiment with toddlers in which they dropped an object on the floor up to fifteen times and found that each time the toddler would pick it up and hand it back. In one part of the experiment, researchers dropped a spoon into a box and pretended they could not get it out. Researchers never asked children for help or rewarded them for helping, but all of the children in the study helped the researcher, usually within ten seconds. They were willing and able to help spontaneously. Further, when the researchers purposely threw something on the floor, the infants could figure out in which situation help was really needed to pick it up and when it was not.[2] That is particularly telling because it shows that even infants and toddlers possess the ability to distinguish between nuances involved in helping others. Overall the researchers concluded that altruistic behaviors are present in young children from the beginning— and that these behaviors are strengthened or reduced based on what is reinforced by their environment.

Sadly, our world doesn't always reinforce acts of altruism and selflessness. These characteristics often take a backseat to more self-centered desires, such as our drive for success, or media and cultural pressures that focus on fulfilling our own needs before those of others. In today's fast-paced world, we are driven to get ahead. It is critical to counteract that with nurturing empathy and altruism in our youth. If we weren't so lucky to have it reinforced as children, we can change. We can work on developing this skill, become a great example of kindness, and be someone who values social connections while giving freely to others.

While altruistic or empathetic people ask for no payback, they do reap benefits for their kindness. My husband and I met because he helped a mom care for her epileptic child on a plane without any expectations—and to cut a long, amazing story short, he was introduced to me through them several years later by chance. Life works in mysterious ways if you open yourself to it. Plus research has shown that acts of kindness and generosity spread easily; it only takes a few people to make a difference and start the domino effect.[3] Now, that's something to feel really good about and empowered by.

Take Stock

It's important to check in with yourself and evaluate your level of altruism. Be really honest and answer purely about how you currently behave, not how you *want* to behave.

Do you like helping out friends and family? YES NO

Would you return a lost wallet full of cash to the rightful owner without any expectation of reward? YES NO

Are you one of the first people to raise a hand to help out for community, school, or work functions? YES NO

Do you contribute—financially or with your time—to worthy causes? YES NO

When you have a full cart of groceries and someone behind you in the checkout line has only a few items, do you let them cut in front of you? YES NO

Do you cringe when kids are next to you
in an airplane, or do you feel for their parents,
who have to juggle them on the flight?   YES NO

Do you offer to help people out when
they're in a bind?   YES NO

Are you one of the first to help a friend
in need?   YES NO

If you answered no to a lot of these questions, you need an empathy reboot. Empathy is in there somewhere, but it's buried. Let's get it out.

Daily Dos

Morning: Your task today is to do one kind, helpful, unexpected thing for someone without wanting anything in return. Be honest with yourself, and really work on that second part. Write down what you're going to do, when, and for whom. If you can't think of anyone right away, start by writing down the names of some people in your life who have been most helpful to you. They're a good place to start. Over time, you will see that you start doing this more naturally, and perhaps you will do it more than once per day and to many other people. You will see your well-being improve, as well as your health, happiness, and resilience. Notice how you feel, and write it down.

Day: Of course giving to others is an important part of growing altruism. But take the extra step to challenge yourself and give in a way that builds upon what you're already good at. For example, if you are a singer or love to sing in a choir, go to a local nursing home or mental health facility and offer to sing for an hour. If you're good at baking or crafts, try making holiday baked goods or gift baskets at a local food bank. If you love food (or you're just good at eating it), buy a little extra for the homeless man on your street. The next time you're cooking, make extra to give to a local shelter. It doesn't take much, but it'll do wonders in increasing your happiness and ultimately your resilience, too.

Night: Keep a journal to jot down your acts of kindness. Be very specific, so things don't start to blend together and get muddled in your mind. Make sure to write down exactly what your good deeds were and how you felt both before and after. The act of writing confirms the good that you have brought to someone's day and in turn makes *you* feel good. The journal can also serve as a pick-me-up whenever you are feeling down—it can be uplifting to remember all the good you have done for others.

Lifelong: Altruism is a lifelong practice. Studies have found that people were more likely to help someone after they had been prompted to think about a caring figure or a caring gesture.[4] Psychologists have termed this concept "priming." By activating particular associations, we are more likely to behave in a related way because our brain is already in that headspace. For example, if a person sees the color red and then is asked what fruits he likes best, he's more likely to choose a red-colored fruit because his memory of red has been triggered.

To start, find a time each day, preferably in the morning since it will prime you to be more helpful as you go about your day. You only need about two minutes. Visualize helping someone in need by creating a mental picture of what it would look like—it can be someone you know or a stranger. You might see yourself helping an elderly person load groceries, or perhaps it is a person at work who needs a good mentor. So the next time you have the opportunity to do an altruistic act, you will be more inclined to do it—because that area of your brain has been awakened to the concept. By keeping altruistic thoughts at the top of your mind, you will be prone to behaving with empathy and altruism. Good deeds will increase your sense of connectivity to others, help you appreciate your life and be more grateful, boost self-respect, make you feel more useful—and ultimately, more resilient.

Gratitude

....

*Do not spoil what you have by desiring what you have
not; remember that what you now have was once among
the things you only hoped for.*

EPICURUS

I'm going out on a limb and saying that gratitude is courageous. Gratitude is related to improved health, greater happiness, better relationships, less anxiety and depression, and
lower stress levels,[1] all of which increase resilience. But I also
say "courageous" because it's easy to go through life on autopilot, expecting certain things to happen and letting other things
pass as time goes by. It takes specific awareness and fortitude
to break the monotony and consciously give thanks for our
blessings. Having said that, people who aren't grateful can still
live rather well. It's easy to expect to wake up in the morning, expect that your family is healthy, expect that you'll still

have your job if you work hard enough, and that your friends will support you if you're a good friend as well. But when we bravely adopt an attitude of gratitude, we catapult out of our status quo and with it improve our quality of life and resilience dramatically.

We enjoy life more when we are reminded about how much goodness we possess. We don't wallow in our sorrow. We are motivated by gratitude to have positive feelings and to persevere. Gratitude makes us appreciate what we have instead of focusing on what we don't have. In that way, we are more motivated to rebound from a crisis when we feel as if we have a good life to rebound to (or toward). Gratitude also has been shown to improve our physical and emotional health[2]—a stronger body and mind bolster our ability to process stress more productively.

A recent study conducted among university students looked at significant predictors of resilience. More than 160 students completed the surveys, and the results showed that of all the predictors, gratitude was most highly tied to resilience, and that was followed by forgiveness and acceptance.[3] While this relies on a student population, it's still very telling.

Why is that? An awareness of what's good in our lives, even if we have to dig deep to see it, propels us to push through challenges and cultivate resilience. Studies have shown that gratitude is so powerful in fact that, in one longitudinal study of more than 200 people using a variety of self-report questionnaires, high levels of gratitude and grit correlated with a reduction in suicidal thoughts over a one-month period to nearly zero. Researchers in this study note that these two factors bolster resilience to suicide by increasing meaning of life. Gratitude can be that potent.[4]

And while we know how healthful and resilience-promoting gratitude can be, it's important to avoid beating yourself up for not always feeling grateful. Feelings of gratitude are emotions just like other emotions such as sadness, fear, happiness, and anger. You're not going to always feel the same way, just as you're not always going to feel thankful, and that's okay. If you practice gratitude, eventually you'll start to feel appreciative, which will promote other benefits as well. But the key is that it'll come and go like all other things and to accept that without being so hard on yourself.

I hear people say a lot that they are grateful in hindsight, which seems to be part of the human condition. We appreciate what occurred after the fact mostly because we're too invested in the feelings of that moment, good or bad, which often prevents us from also feeling thankful. Unless we've practiced making gratitude a part of our lives consistently, it's hard for it to be ever-present. While being grateful is good for us no matter when we feel it, resilient people *decide* to be grateful—and are able to weave gratitude into their lives every day to make it a bit more effortless.

Take Stock

....

Let's assess where you are with gratitude.

Is it hard for you to think of things you're thankful for?

NEVER/OCCASIONALLY/FREQUENTLY/ALWAYS

Do you often send thank-you notes or express gratitude?

NEVER/OCCASIONALLY/FREQUENTLY/ALWAYS

Do you do small acts of kindness for those who have been helpful to you, such as bringing a colleague lunch so he can keep working on a project or getting mail for neighbors when they're on vacation?

NEVER/OCCASIONALLY/FREQUENTLY/ALWAYS

Are you grateful when you wake up for your day?

NEVER/OCCASIONALLY/FREQUENTLY/ALWAYS

Do you find yourself taking a moment to appreciate a happy moment?

NEVER/OCCASIONALLY/FREQUENTLY/ALWAYS

Are you surrounded by others who are grateful?

NEVER/OCCASIONALLY/FREQUENTLY/ALWAYS

If you created a list of what you're grateful for, it would be a really long one.

STRONGLY AGREE/AGREE/DISAGREE/STRONGLY DISAGREE

If gratitude isn't part of daily life, there are ways to work on that, which I have outlined below.

Would you like to become more grateful, and if so, how do you see gratitude making a positive change in your life?

_____

_____

_____

_____

_____

Daily Dos

Morning: Complaining is commonplace. But it's lazy and a poor way to procrastinate. It does very little to remedy or improve; it's inactive vocalization of issues. Choose one hour today in which you're not going to complain about anything, internally or externally. Internally is the harder part. You are going to accept that hour as it is and be mindful of your reactions to things and your experience. We often complain without even realizing it, and it's so accepted and routine that it has become a large part of our internal dialogue. This complaining mentality gets in the way of gratitude. We automatically find so much wrong in the world that we have a harder time seeing what's right with it. If one hour is too hard for you, that's okay. The important part is that you try. Then give yourself thirty minutes to start. Slowly you'll find yourself increasing the time commitment. Wouldn't it be wonderful if you could get through a whole day without once complaining, to yourself or to others? Your resilience and health would flourish.

Day: Act on your gratitude. It's important to not just think about being grateful but also to show gratitude to others. True gratitude is an action as much as it is a feeling. Doing something that expresses gratitude improves relationships dramatically and boosts positive feelings, and thus increases quality of life. Do something to show someone you're grateful for them. Give a hug. Hugging has been shown in the research to protect the heart,[5] increase feelings of joy, and even improve immunity to illness.[6] Say thank you to the cashier at the store, or do something helpful for a friend during a tough time. I still remember those friends who brought me dinner after I had given birth. They didn't have to say anything, but I felt their love and gratitude through their action of being helpful when I needed it. It can also be as simple as sending a letter to a partner or friend to share appreciation, or including a note in your children's backpack. A handwritten letter goes a long way in this age of technology because it's so rare, but if you don't have time for that, an e-mail or a text is great, too. A Facebook or Instagram comment is fine as well, but they're so plentiful that they often aren't as fulfilling. Small acts can be deeply meaningful—you don't always have to verbally say "thank you." You can also *show* appreciation through being a good listener to a colleague who has been good to you, or bringing back an extra coffee for him or her when you're out getting one for yourself. This is also very helpful to do when you've run into a rough patch with someone you care about. Challenging yourself to find something to appreciate in them, and doing something that shows that gratitude will help you both move forward.

Night: Do a gratitude pause before going to sleep. This doesn't have to take long, but it can be very effective. Let yourself lie quietly and comfortably. Breathe normally. Acknowledge yourself and your day. Be grateful for your mind and well-being, for your health, for your friends and family, and for the lessons you've learned that day. If you have had a difficult time learning from your hardships, use this quiet moment to mentally see the challenge before you and focus on what you can learn. There's always something. This will help you reframe the way you look at your daily challenges (as opportunities perhaps rather than just negative experiences) and will help clear your mind so you are able to move forward constructively.

Lifelong: You've probably heard about the power of gratitude journals. But don't just do it the traditional way. Research has shown that gratitude journals do indeed have a significant effect on our health and happiness if done right. Instead of just jotting down a couple of things you're grateful for, challenge yourself to write down at least three significant *new* things that you're grateful for every day, and make them profound; be specific and dig deeper—if it's your kids, don't just write "my kids." What specifically are you grateful for? That your kids are developing into respectful people? That they helped you with cleanup after dinner? Did you tell them that you were grateful? This journal is your mirror, your reflection tool. Use it wisely.

Don't just repeat gratitudes. Try to find novel things every day. Writing it out will also make you recognize what gratitude feels like and work on how to properly express it. This can be done in the same journal you used for your altruism notes, but make sure you have separate sections for each. This is a great way to build upon gratitude long-term and will also be a useful tool to help you evaluate your progress, as you will be able to look back at all your multitude of blessings. Start small, and soon you'll find your gratitude will flow. Be careful not to be too hard on yourself about this. People sometimes feel too much pressure to be grateful or can't find the words to express their gratitude. It's normal for it to be rather hard to do at first. Over time, approaching life from a thankful place will strengthen your ability to live with resilience.

Daily Log

Use the tracker below to check off your daily dos and add notes to track your feelings, thoughts, and accomplishments

Week 1 Self   Notes

Day 1	**Habit**	○ Morning	○ Day	○ Evening
Day 2	**Hope**	○ Morning	○ Day	○ Evening
Day 3	**Health**	○ Morning	○ Day	○ Evening
Day 4	**Control**	○ Morning	○ Day	○ Evening
Day 5	**Playfulness**	○ Morning	○ Day	○ Evening
Day 6	**Self-Respect**	○ Morning	○ Day	○ Evening
Day 7	**Self-Awareness**	○ Morning	○ Day	○ Evening

Week 2 Spirit

Day 8	**Realistic Optimism**	○ Morning	○ Day	○ Evening
Day 9	**Mindfulness**	○ Morning	○ Day	○ Evening
Day 10	**Integrity**	○ Morning	○ Day	○ Evening
Day 11	**Spirituality**	○ Morning	○ Day	○ Evening
Day 12	**Flexibility**	○ Morning	○ Day	○ Evening
Day 13	**Perseverance**	○ Morning	○ Day	○ Evening
Day 14	**Acceptance**	○ Morning	○ Day	○ Evening

Week 3 Social

Day 15	**Innovation**	○ Morning	○ Day	○ Evening
Day 16	**Emotional Intelligence**	○ Morning	○ Day	○ Evening
Day 17	**Purpose**	○ Morning	○ Day	○ Evening
Day 18	**Problem Solving**	○ Morning	○ Day	○ Evening
Day 19	**Social Connectivity**	○ Morning	○ Day	○ Evening
Day 20	**Altruism**	○ Morning	○ Day	○ Evening
Day 21	**Gratitude**	○ Morning	○ Day	○ Evening

Afterword

....

The thing that is really hard, and really amazing,
is giving up on being perfect and beginning
the work of becoming yourself.

ANNA QUINDLEN

Belief is incredibly powerful. When we believe in something, for right or wrong, it becomes our truth. Positive, goal-oriented beliefs—that you can achieve success, that you can be happy, that you can do what you set out to do, that you can bounce back from adversity—set the foundation for your life.

I recently came across a fascinating study that, by interpreting brain images, showed how people perceive and treat their future selves differently from their present selves. In the study, participants were asked to think of themselves in ten years, and in that moment their brain activity was the same as when they were thinking of strangers.[1] The only way we can really know a person is by experiencing their actions and behaviors, and since we haven't done that with our future selves, we have some familiarity but no authentic connection.

This becomes tricky when we make choices for the future; we are doing so without knowing much about who we're going to become, let alone feeling any connection to that person. So how can we possibly make good decisions for ourselves long-term, decisions that empower us and increase resilience? A good way to overcome this disconnect is to act as if your future self is someone you really care about and want to treat well, like your best friend. Act as if you really love the future, resilient person you're becoming—you will rebound more easily and build your resilience more than you would have otherwise.

Hopefully at this point in the book you feel well equipped to overcome adversity and also to grow from it. I've highlighted throughout the importance of remaining positive with whatever comes your way. It is indeed of utmost significance, and plays a large role in well-being. However, remaining positive is not a direct path to happiness. The problem today is that people are inundated with being told to "think positive," so they've become *afraid* of the negative. They mistake happiness for only feeling happy thoughts and feelings, and they confuse resilience for never truly experiencing pain. You now know that's not what any of this is about. We can't escape the daily grind. But we can use stress to our advantage; it can actually be motivating and adaptive if we react to it effectively.

Our most trying moments are valuable teachers—as resilient people, we must expect to learn from them. While this foreknowledge won't take away the pain of those moments or experiences, knowing in advance that we will come out of it stronger reduces some of the sting.

We all have the power to be our strongest, most resilient version of ourselves. You made a choice to be that person when you started reading this book. I hope you take the skills you've learned, practice them, and build on them. You're worth it.

Acknowledgments

....

We can only be said to be alive in those moments
when our hearts are conscious of our treasures.

THORNTON WILDER

Writing this book has been an extraordinary journey. I'm profoundly thankful to so many people in my life who have been a
constant source of encouragement. This could not have come
to fruition without you, and I'm thrilled to have an opportunity
to officially thank you on these pages.

Deepest gratitude to my phenomenal agent, Meg Thompson, and to all at Thompson Literary Agency who supported
this book. Meg, thank you for believing in me. You have never
wavered; your loyalty and perseverance have been founda-
tional, always giving consistently sound advice with my best
interests at heart. Thanks also to Kathryn Huck, whose expertise I relied on tremendously.

I owe an incalculable debt of gratitude to my brilliant editor, Gideon Weil. Without you, this book wouldn't exist. Our synergy was instantaneous from the moment we first spoke. Honoring my voice above all else and responding to every inquiry with the most gracious consideration, you've been a dream to work with. Many thanks also to the talented team at HarperElixir, including my esteemed publisher Claudia Boutote, as well as the admirable Hilary Lawson, Lisa Zuniga, Suzanne Wickham, Adia Colar, and Ann Edwards, whose commitment to me, and this book, has been truly humbling. I'm deeply grateful to all of you for your skillful guidance and unwavering encouragement.

To my sincere, thoughtful friends, you are my web of support. From giving me the space I needed for writing while still checking in, to insisting on throwing my son's birthday party because I had deadlines to meet, to putting up with my psychological banter, to never taking anything (including out-of-character last-minute cancellations!) personally, and for much more, I am so thankful. I also want to extend utmost gratitude to my current YPO forum group for always being such genuine allies and mentors. Each of you is extremely meaningful to me.

My family has been a fundamental source of fortitude. Thank you for being such consistent cheerleaders. Special gratitude to my husband's family and my selfless mother-in-law, Carmen Montminy, for your unabating helpfulness. Your resilience, altruism, and joie de vivre are truly inspirational.

Heartfelt thanks to my sister, Fianna Jurdant, and her family, for your unmitigated devotion and insight. I cherish you with all my heart. You've always been by my side, although physically far, and are a constant source of unconditional love and reassurance. You and your confidence in me are an invaluable gift.

My most sincere appreciation goes to my loving parents, Efim and Esfira Muchnik. I am so proud of your journey. You set the foundation for my resilience by living with determination and endurance. I am forever grateful for you and your resourcefulness, generosity, and cultivation. To thank you for everything isn't enough.

To my dear husband, Joel, from the moment we first met on our blind date, and still today, you are the one. You are my pulse, as it's engraved in our wedding rings, *mo chuisle*. Our love and your tenacity are my strength; you inspire me every day. Thank you for your perpetual faith and tireless dedication to our family. My fantasies pale in comparison to the life we've created together.

Ethan and Ava, my precious children, you are now three and one. You're my power source, and have been empathetic and adaptive even at such a young age. You are both so brave. Your joy and vitality remind me daily of all that is right, of all that is good. May you always see the world with the same wonder as you do today. In the most turbulent of times, and most magical of times, you have enriched my life with such meaning, depth, and devotion that I never knew existed. Thank you for being my greatest teachers.

Notes

Introduction

1. Iris B. Mauss et al., "Can Seeking Happiness Make People Unhappy? Paradoxical Effects of Valuing Happiness," *Emotion* 11, no. 4 (2011): 807; Pelin Kesebir and Ed Diener, "In Pursuit of Happiness: Empirical Answers to Philosophical Questions," *Perspectives on Psychological Science* 3, no. 2 (2008): 117–25.
2. June Gruber, Iris B. Mauss, and Maya Tamir, "A Dark Side of Happiness? How, When, and Why Happiness Is Not Always Good," *Perspectives on Psychological Science* 6, no. 3 (2011): 222–33.
3. Iris B. Mauss et al., "The Pursuit of Happiness Can Be Lonely," *Emotion* 12, no. 5 (2012), 908.
4. Julia Kim-Cohen et al., "Genetic and Environmental Processes in Young Children's Resilience and Vulnerability to Socioeconomic Deprivation," *Child Development* 75, no. 3 (2004): 651–68.
5. Michele M. Tugade, Barbara L. Fredrickson, and Lisa Feldman Barrett, "Psychological Resilience and Positive Emotional Granularity: Examining the Benefits of Positive Emotions on Coping and Health," *Journal of Personality* 72, no. 6 (2004): 1161–90.
6. Barbara L. Fredrickson, Michele M. Tugade, Christian E. Waugh, and Gregory R. Larkin, "What Good Are Positive Emotions in Crises? A Prospective Study of Resilience and Emotions Following the Terrorist Attacks on the United States on September 11th, 2001," *Journal of Personality and Social Psychology* 84, no. 2 (2003): 365–76.
7. P. Lally, C. H. M. van Jaarsveld, H. W. W. Potts, and J. Wardle, "How Are Habits Formed? Modelling Habit Formation in the Real World," *European Journal of Social Psychology* 40 (2010): 998–1009.
8. Lally, "How Are Habits Formed."

Day 1: Habit

1. Wendy Wood, "Habits in Everyday Life: How to Form Good Habits and Change Bad Ones," August 7, 2014, American Psychological Association's 122nd Annual Convention, Washington, D.C.

2. Judith A. Ouellette and Wendy Wood, "Habit and Intention in Everyday Life: The Multiple Processes by Which Past Behavior Predicts Future Behavior," *Psychological Bulletin* 124, no. 1 (July 1998): 54–74.
3. Wendy Wood, Jeffrey M. Quinn, and Deborah A. Kashy, "Habits in Everyday Life: Thought, Emotion, and Action," *Journal of Personality and Social Psychology* 83, no. 6 (December 2002): 1281–97.
4. Liz Welch, "David Karp: The Nonconformist Who Built Tumblr," Inc .com, June 2001, www.inc.com/magazine/201106/the-way-i-work -david-karp-of-tumblr.html.
5. Oprah Winfrey, "What Oprah Knows for Sure About Finding the Fullest Expression of Yourself," Oprah.com, February 2012, www.oprah .com /health/Oprah-on-Stillness-and-Meditation-Oprah-Visits-Fairfield -Iowa#ixzz3WHbySJPP.
6. Christopher Clarey, "Olympians Use Imagery as Mental Training," *New York Times*, February 22, 2014, www.nytimes.com/2014/02/23/sports /olympics/olympians-use-imagery-as-mental-training.html?_r=0.
7. Charles Duhigg, "How You Can Harness 'The Power of Habit,'" NPR.org, February 27, 2012, www.npr.org/2012/02/27/147296743/how-you-can -harness-the-power-of-habit; Wendy Wood and David T. Neal, "A New Look at Habits and the Habit-Goal Interface," *Psychological Review* 114, no. 4 (October 2007): 843–63.
8. Theresa M. Desrochers, Dezhe Z. Jin, Noah D. Goodman, and Ann M. Graybiel, "Optimal Habits Can Develop Spontaneously Through Sensitivity to Local Cost," *Proceedings of the National Academy of Sciences* 107, no. 47 (November 2010): 20512–17.
9. David T. Neal, Wendy Wood, and Jeffrey M. Quinn, "Habits: A Repeat Performance," *Association for Psychological Science* 15, no. 4 (2006): 198–202.

Day 2: Hope

1. E. D. Raleigh, "Sources of Hope in Chronic Illness," *Oncology Nursing Forum* 19, no. 3 (1992).
2. Claude M. Steele, "The Psychology of Self-Affirmation: Sustaining the Integrity of the Self," *Advances in Experimental Social Psychology* 21, no. 2 (1988): 261–302.
3. Jennifer S. Cheavens, Scott T. Michael, C. R. Snyder, and Jaklin A. Eliott (eds.), "The Correlates of Hope: Psychological and Physiological Benefits," *Interdisciplinary Perspectives on Hope* XII.296 (2005): 119–32.
4. Edward C. Chang, "Hope, Problem-Solving Ability, and Coping in a College Student Population: Some Implications for Theory and Practice," *Journal of Clinical Psychology* 54, no. 7 (1998): 953–62.

Notes

5. Lewis A. Curry et al., "Role of Hope in Academic and Sport Achievement," *Journal of Personality and Social Psychology* 73, no. 6 (1997): 1257.
6. M. Watson et al., "Influence of Psychological Response on Breast Cancer Survival: 10-Year Follow-Up of a Population-Based Cohort," *European Journal of Cancer* 41, no. 12 (2005): 1710–14.
7. Michael A. Cohn et al., "Happiness Unpacked: Positive Emotions Increase Life Satisfaction by Building Resilience," *Emotion* 9, no. 3 (2009): 361.

Day 3: Health

1. R. J. Schloesser et al., "Environmental Enrichment Requires Adult Neurogenesis to Facilitate the Recovery from Psychosocial Stress," *Molecular Psychiatry* 15, no. 12 (2010): 1152–63.

Day 4: Control

1. Alex Korb, *The Upward Spiral: Using Neuroscience to Reverse the Course of Depression, One Small Change at a Time* (Oakland, CA: New Harbinger Publications, 2015).
2. Ellen J. Langer, *Counterclockwise: Mindful Health and the Power of Possibility* (New York: Ballantine Books, 2009).
3. Jan Gläscher et al., "Lesion Mapping of Cognitive Control and Value-Based Decision Making in the Prefrontal Cortex," *Proceedings of the National Academy of Sciences* 109, no. 36 (2012): 14681–86.

Day 5: Playfulness

1. Ramon Mora-Ripoll, "The Therapeutic Value of Laughter in Medicine," *Alternative Therapies in Health and Medicine* 16, no. 6 (2010): 56–64.
2. *Humor—International Journal of Humor Research* 15, no. 4 (February 2008): 365–81, ISSN (online) 1613–3722, ISSN (print) 0933–1719, doi: 10.1515/humr.15.4.365.
3. Viktor E. Frankl, *Man's Search for Meaning* (New York: Simon and Schuster, 1985).
4. Robert R. Provine, "Contagious Laughter: Laughter Is a Sufficient Stimulus for Laughs and Smiles," *Bulletin of Psychonomic Society* 30, no. 1 (July 1992): 1–4.

Day 6: Self-Respect

1. Zuzana Veselska et al., "Self-Esteem and Resilience," *Addictive Behaviors Journal* 34, no. 3 (March 2009): 287–91.

2. P. Briñol, R. E. Petty, and B. Wagner, "Body Posture Effects on Self-Evaluation: A Self-Validation Approach," *European Journal of Social Psychology* 39 (2009): 1053–64.
3. Dana R. Carney, Amy J. C. Cuddy, and Andy J. Yap, "Power Posing: Brief Nonverbal Displays Affect Neuroendocrine Levels and Risk Tolerance," *Psychological Science* 21, no. 10 (2010): 1363–68.

Day 7: Self-Awareness

1. William John Ickes, Robert A. Wicklund, and C. Brian Ferris, "Objective Self Awareness and Self Esteem," *Journal of Experimental Social Psychology* 9, no. 3 (1973): 202–19.

Day 8: Realistic Optimism

1. Alex J. Zautra, *Emotions, Stress, and Health* (New York: Oxford Univ. Press, 2006).
2. Christopher Peterson, "The Future of Optimism," *American Psychologist* 55, no. 1 (2000): 44.
3. Etty Hillesum, Klaas A. D. Smelik, and Arnold Pomerans, *Etty: The Letters and Diaries of Etty Hillesum, 1941–1943* (Cambridge: Wm. B. Eerdmans Publishing, 2002).
4. Lynn A. Jansen et al., "Unrealistic Optimism in Early-Phase Oncology Trials," *IRB* 33, no. 1 (2011): 1–8.
5. Alex Korb, *The Upward Spiral: Using Neuroscience to Reverse the Course of Depression, One Small Change at a Time* (Oakland, CA: New Harbinger Publications, 2015.
6. Paul Ekman and Richard J. Davidson, "Voluntary Smiling Changes Regional Brain Activity," *Psychological Science* 4, no. 5 (1993): 342–45.
7. P. Briñol, R. E. Petty, and B. Wagner, "Body Posture Effects on Self-Evaluation: A Self-Validation Approach," *European Journal of Social Psychology* 39 (2009): 1053–64.

Day 9: Mindfulness

1. Rachel W. Thompson, Diane B. Arnkoff, and Carol R. Glass, "Conceptualizing Mindfulness and Acceptance as Components of Psychological Resilience to Trauma," *Trauma, Violence, & Abuse* 12, no. 4 (2011): 220–35.
2. David M. Levy et al., "The Effects of Mindfulness Meditation Training on Multitasking in a High-Stress Information Environment," *Proceedings of Graphics Interface 2012*, Canadian Information Processing Society.

3. Alia J. Crum, Peter Salovey, and Shawn Achor, "Rethinking Stress: The Role of Mindsets in Determining the Stress Response," *Journal of Personality and Social Psychology* 104, no. 4 (2013): 716.
4. Elisha David Goldstein, "Sacred Moments: Implications on Well-Being and Stress," *Journal of Clinical Psychology* 63, no. 10 (2007): 1001–19.
5. Richard J. Davidson et al., "Alterations in Brain and Immune Function Produced by Mindfulness Meditation," *Psychosomatic Medicine* 65, no. 4 (2003): 564–70.

Day 10: Integrity

1. Anne Frank, *The Diary of a Young Girl* (New York: Doubleday, 1991).
2. Carola Wärnå, Lisbet Lindholm, and Katie Eriksson, "Virtue and Health: Finding Meaning and Joy in Working Life," *Scandinavian Journal of Caring Sciences* 21, no. 2 (2007): 191–98.

Day 11: Spirituality

1. Peter C. Hill and Kenneth I. Pargament, "Advances in the Conceptualization and Measurement of Religion and Spirituality: Implications for Physical and Mental Health Research," *Psychology of Religion and Spirituality* S(1) (August 2008): 3–17.
2. Prem S. Fry, "Religious Involvement, Spirituality and Personal Meaning for Life: Existential Predictors of Psychological Wellbeing in Community-Residing and Institutional Care Elders," *Aging & Mental Health* 4, no. 4 (2000): 375–87.
3. Harold G. Koenig, "Religion, Spirituality, and Health: The Research and Clinical Implications," *ISRN Psychiatry* (2012).

Day 12: Flexibility

1. Christian E. Waugh, Renee J. Thompson, and Ian H. Gotlib, "Flexible Emotional Responsiveness in Trait Resilience," *Emotion* 11, no. 5 (2011): 1059.
2. Alan Rozanski and Laura D. Kubzansky, "Psychologic Functioning and Physical Health: A Paradigm of Flexibility," *Psychosomatic Medicine* 67 (2005): S47–S53.

Day 14: Acceptance

1. Alex Korb, *The Upward Spiral: Using Neuroscience to Reverse the Course of Depression, One Small Change at a Time* (Oakland, CA: New Harbinger Publications, 2015.

2. Kalman J. Kaplan, "From Attitude Formation to Attitude Change: Acceptance and Impact as Cognitive Mediators," *Sociometry* (1972): 448–67.

Day 16: Emotional Intelligence

1. M. M. Tugade and B. L. Fredrickson, "Resilient Individuals Use Positive Emotions to Bounce Back from Negative Emotional Experiences," *Journal of Personality and Social Psychology* 86, no. 2 (2004): 320–33.
2. Matthew D. Lieberman et al., "Putting Feelings into Words: Affect Labeling Disrupts Amygdala Activity in Response to Affective Stimuli," *Psychological Science* 18, no. 5 (2007): 421–28.
3. M. M. Tugade, B. L. Fredrickson, and Barrett L. Feldman, "Psychological Resilience and Positive Emotional Granularity: Examining the Benefits of Positive Emotions on Coping and Health," *Journal of Personality* 72, no. 6 (2004): 1162–90.

Day 17: Purpose

1. E. S. Kim, J. K. Sun, N. Park, and C. Peterson, "Purpose in Life and Reduced Stroke in Older Adults: The Health and Retirement Study," *Journal of Psychosomatic Research* 74, no. 5 (May 2013): 427–32.
2. Rush University Medical Center, "Purpose in Life and Alzheimer's: Researchers Identify a Potential Protector," www.rush.edu/health-wellness/discover-health/purpose-life-and-alzheimers.
3. Bruce W. Smith et al., "The Role of Resilience and Purpose in Life in Habituation to Heat and Cold Pain," *Journal of Pain* 10, no. 5 (2009): 493–500.

Day 18: Problem Solving

1. Fikret Berkes, "Understanding Uncertainty and Reducing Vulnerability: Lessons from Resilience Thinking," *Natural Hazards* 41, no. 2 (2007): 283–95.
2. Mehmet Eskin, "Resilience, Coping, and Problem Solving," *Problem Solving Therapy in the Clinical Practice* (2013): 9–16.
3. Alex Korb, *The Upward Spiral: Using Neuroscience to Reverse the Course of Depression, One Small Change at a Time* (Oakland, CA: New Harbinger Publications, 2015).

Notes

Day 19: Social Connectivity

1. F. Ozbay, H. Fitterling, D. Charney, and S. Southwick, "Social Support and Resilience to Stress Across the Life Span: A Neurobiologic Framework," *Current Psychiatry Report* 10, no. 4 (August 2008): 304–10.
2. Sofie Vanassche, Gray Swicegood, and Koen Matthijs, "Marriage and Children as a Key to Happiness? Cross-National Differences in the Effects of Marital Status and Children on Well-Being," *Journal of Happiness Studies* 14, no. 2 (2013): 501–24.

Day 20: Altruism

1. C. Schwartz, news release, Health Behavior News Service, *Psychosomatic Medicine* 65 (September/October 2003).
2. Felix Warneken and Michael Tomasello, "Altruistic Helping in Human Infants and Young Chimpanzees," *Science* 311, no. 5766 (March 2006): 1301–3, www.sciencemag.org/content/311/5765/1301.abstract.
3. James H. Fowler and Nicholas A. Christakis, "Cooperative Behavior Cascades in Human Social Networks," *Proceedings of the National Academy of Sciences* 107, no. 12 (March 2010): 5334–38.
4. Mario Mikulincer et al., "Attachment, Caregiving, and Altruism: Boosting Attachment Security Increases Compassion and Helping," *Journal of Personality and Social Psychology* 89, no. 5 (2005): 817.

Day 21: Gratitude

1. Alex M. Wood, Jeffrey J. Froh, and Adam W. A. Geraghty, "Gratitude and Well-Being: A Review and Theoretical Integration," *Clinical Psychology Review* 30, no. 7 (2010): 890–905.
2. Robert A. Emmons and Michael E. McCullough, "Counting Blessings Versus Burdens: An Experimental Investigation of Gratitude and Subjective Well-Being in Daily Life," *Journal of Personality and Social Psychology* 84, no. 2 (2003): 377.
3. Hal Ersner-Hershfield, G. Elliott Wimmer, and Brian Knutson, "Saving for the Future Self: Neural Measures of Future Self-Continuity Predict Temporal Discounting," *Social Cognitive and Affective Neuroscience* 4.1 (2009): 85–92.
4. Evan M. Kleiman et al., "Gratitude and Grit Indirectly Reduce Risk of Suicidal Ideations by Enhancing Meaning in Life: Evidence for a Mediated Moderation Model," *Journal of Research in Personality* 47, no. 5 (2013): 539–46.

5. Sheldon Cohen et al., "Does Hugging Provide Stress-Buffering Social Support: A Study of Susceptibility to Upper Respiratory Infection and Illness," *Psychological Sciences* 26, no. 2 (2015): 135–47.
6. Kathleen C. Light, Karen M. Grewen, and Janet A. Amico, "More Frequent Partner Hugs and Higher Oxytocin Levels Are Linked to Lower Blood Pressure and Heart Rate in Premenopausal Women," *Biological Psychology* 69, no. 1 (2005): 5–21.